A TIME OF TURMOIL

A TIME OF TURMOIL

Values and Voting in the 1970's

RONALD R. STOCKTON

FRANK WHELON WAYMAN

THE MICHIGAN STATE UNIVERSITY PRESS
East Lansing

Library of Congress Cataloging in Publication Data
Stockton, Ronald R.
    A time of turmoil.
    1. Public opinion—Michigan—Dearborn—
Longitudinal studies.   2. Presidents—
United States—Election—1972.
3. Presidents—United States—Election—
1976.
I.   Wayman, Frank Whelon.   II.   Title
HN90.P8S86   1983
324.973′092
82-61713
ISBN 0-87013-232-6

Distributed by Wayne State University Press
Detroit, Michigan 48202

*
 *
*
 *
  *

To Ellen and Jane

Preface

This is a book on public opinion in the 1970's. It is an effort to describe, from the perspective of one community, the impact which those opinions had upon voting in the two presidential elections of the 1970's. It will show how values and attitudes are structured and how a shifting emphasis in the voters' minds led to dramtically different outcomes and voting patterns in the 1972 and 1976 elections. At the heart of our research is a question which scholars and observers alike have been asking for well over a decade without a satisfactory answer: are the concerns of voters and the attachment of voters to parties changing in such a way as to produce a realignment of the political system? Our data show more evidence of disintegration than of realignment, but like others we will have to put a "wait and see" caveat into our conclusions.

The focus of our study is Dearborn, Michigan, a city which our research shows was representative of much that was happening in northern urban white America. For decades a typical urban Democratic stronghold, by the late sixties Dearborn began to show all the inconsistencies of national politics. In 1968 it gained national attention as the first community in the country to pass an anti-war referendum, even as it was emerging as a center of pro-Wallace sentiment. It reacted with near-panic to the Detroit riots of 1967, and played a major role in the anti-busing movement of 1973. Its colorful and very popular mayor of over 30 years was an outspoken segregationist even as he endorsed social welfare programs and renounced the war. The recession of 1973 and the economic malaise which lasted throughout the decade undermined the self-confidence of the early 1960's and subjected the city to the economic and social pressures so typical of the 1970's. We began and concluded the study fascinated by this community.

The data used in the study consist of a panel of 801 Dearborn residents. A panel study has advantages over an ordinary public opinion poll in that the same people are interviewed several times, in this case on four different occasions between 1974 and 1976. By reinterviewing the same respondents and repeating some of the same questions from interview to interview, we are able to trace the evolution of opinions and attitudes between the two elections under study. We are also able to see how attitudes towards the parties and major presidential candidates developed during the time of the study. Ironically, the only earlier panel study in American electoral politics based on repeated questions was conducted during a period of stability—the later Eisenhower years—when few shifts in opinion were occurring. Our study offers an uncommon methodology in an uncommon time.

Support for this project came from several sources: data collection was financed by the Rackham Graduate School of the University of Michigan, through its Faculty Research and Fellowship programs. A generous gift from the Ford Motor Company Fund provided timely support for the completion of the project. The Campus Grants Committee of the University of Michigan-Dearborn also made a much-appreciated contribution.

Several individuals deserve personal recognition. Linda Bolton and Fran Featherston were research assistants but contributed far more than that title indicates. Fran's remarkable ability to deal with computers deserves a special mention all its own.

The students in our Political Analysis classes also deserve special commendation. Four tireless cohorts of interviewers swarmed onto the streets year after year, tracking down respondents and recording their views. The high response rate indicates their determination as well as the good-natured cooperation received from the people of Dearborn.

Our wives provided constant encouragement and support.

We are grateful to all of you.

Contents

ONTENTS

CHAPTER 4

The More Things Change, The More They Remain the Same   91
Attitude Changes   92.   Estimating True Change   94.
Patterns of Change   97.   Public Response to Parties,
Leaders, and Issues   99.

CHAPTER 5

The Presidential Elections of 1972 and 1976   105
The 1972 Election   108.   Predicting the 1972 Vote   111.
Analyzing the Results   114.   Response to Watergate   117.
Commitment to Nixon   120.   Belief That the News is Biased   123.
Effects of Political Information   124.   The 1976
Presidential primaries   127.   Candidates and Issues   127.
Candidate Qualities   130.   Issue-Position Images   132.
The Vote   134.   The Power of Party   135.
Perception of the Parties   137.   Economic and Social
Welfare Issues   140.   The 1976 Vote   142.
Issues and the Vote Shift   143.   The Role of Materialism   145.
Predicting the Vote   146.   The Inductive Model:
The Impact of Image   151.   Predicting the Switch   158.

CHAPTER 6

1980 and Beyond   162
The Sundquist Model: An Evaluation   162.
The Future of American Politics   165.

Appendix A: Study Design   168
Appendix B: Questionnaire   170

Notes   188

CHAPTER 1: Party Alignment and Public Opinion

> I can almost smell the disaster mounting invisibly and flood-
> ing out toward me. . . . My hands may perspire, and my
> voice may come out strange. I wonder why. Something must
> have happened to me sometime.
>
> —Joseph Heller
> Something Happened

It became obvious in the mid 1960's that something was happening to America and the American political system. The surface violence was bad enough: three major assassinations, urban riots, the student revolt, and the war in Vietnam. More corrosive was the underlying erosion of national moral fiber, the loss of forward momentum in economic growth, and the decay in the quality of life.

The early 1960's had been an era of unprecedented prosperity. The rich became richer, and so did the poor. It was the time when Americans dreamed of an end to poverty within their lifetimes. It was a time of hope and optimism when Americans turned to their government for leadership, and the government responded with a series of social and economic programs unprecedented in non-emergency times. The promise of the New Frontier was followed by the legislation of the Great Society. It was a time when mortgages were paid off, new homes were built, cars were purchased, children were educated, and plans were laid. The American Dream seemed just around the corner.

But by the end of the decade, many of these hopes had been lost. Homes became insecure as the gap between the poor and the newly affluent middle class sent the crime rate soaring; the war on poverty, like the war in Vietnam, was abandoned as a costly failure; inflation cut into earnings and unemployment became a real concern; racial tensions boiled over into riots, and busing moved school integration north, further threatening the imagined security of the suburbs. Protest groups questioned the very moral position of the nation. The old morality had been threatened at an increasing rate in the 1960's, as the traditional values surrounding school prayer, abortion, drug use, pre-marital sex, and the role of the family came to be more and more in question. "Deviant" groups espousing anti-traditional values were increasingly the object of public and private harassment.

The war in Vietnam also brought into question the credibility of leaders. In the middle 1960's public trust had soared. People believed in public leaders and the ability of government technocrats to govern the country effectively. As the society seemed to disintegrate, leaders came to be more and more in disrepute. The major institutions of society showed marked drops in public trust.[1] The "establishment" became a catchword symbolizing the perceived moral bankruptcy of all national leadership.

A New Value System

These changes produced a new, clearly definable set of values which, to a certain extent, provide a threat to the present political party system. That party system was built on conflicts over New Deal issues such as income maintenance and government regulation of industry.[2] While such issues are still relevant, the new concerns of suburban America at times conflict with or take precedence over the issues of the past. They also cut across party lines and provide a new set of issues that could theoretically lead to a party realignment. In that case, the Democratic sun could set and a Republican sun could rise. Alternately, as a sage observer, Samuel Lubell, put it two decades ago, "American politics may remain the politics of twilight, with the Democratic sun on the wane, but with no new majority sun able to rise to clear ascendancy."[3]

What is this new disruptive system? It is a powerful new value system, not based upon conventional liberal-conservative divisions, but upon a new and stable combination of goals and values. The people with this value system are, first of all, materialistic. They report high levels of personal happiness. They are distrustful, however, of the large institutions around them—especially the government, politicians, and the news media, but also of big business and labor. They are "conservative" in thinking that government programs are wasteful and inefficient. But they are "liberal" on their support of "New Deal" government programs that put money in their pockets: government aid to education, social security, unemployment compensation, medical insurance, and even guaranteed jobs to those who want to work. The people we studied support various aspects of sexual liberation, such as abortion and sex education. In this respect they are liberal. They oppose a variety of other radical or anti-traditional movements: the women's liberation movement, homosexuals, and black militants. In the same vein of conservatism, they support the police, the military, and law and order. The majority are free of classical racial prejudice; they do not think that blacks are genetically inferior. But they have stereotypes of black neighborhoods as dens of crime and vice, and they strongly oppose busing and housing integration.

This new value system is transforming American electoral politics. First, the disruptive "new issues" of the 1960's and 1970's—law and order, abortion, busing, the sexual revolution—cut across the Republican and Democratic party coalitions, and created a potential for party realignment that is still with us. Second, the distrust of institutions, including political parties, creates the potential for a "de-aligned," or "disintegrated" party system. In such a disintegrated system, voters would no longer be very loyal to parties. National leaders would build personal followings based on campaign imagery, and would appeal to the voters directly via the mass media, rather than reaching the voters via the political party organizations. The changing values thus have the potential to realign or de-align the party system. One of the major manifestations of these changes insofar as the political system was concerned occurred in the 1972 election, when the Democratic party disintegrated in a paroxysm of acrimonious conflicts. In a bitter struggle, the McGovern wing of party reformers and war protesters swept the party stalwarts such as Mayor Richard Daley from control of the party.[4] Many old-timers, notably George Meany of the AFL-CIO, walked out of the McGovern campaign that year in a protest of their own. Richard Nixon returned to power with a record-setting 49-state sweep. It seemed to many as if a much anticipated "party realignment"—an epoch-making shift of voters from one party to another— was upon us.[5]

But by 1974 the changing political tides had swept Richard Nixon into exile. In the wake of the Watergate scandal corrupt politicians, businessmen who made illegal campaign contributions, and CIA domestic spies took the place of demonstrators and war protesters as national scapegoats. The Democrats did well in the congressional elec-

13

tions that year, and thereafter had a nearly "veto proof" congress, at least on paper. The talk of realignment continued, but now focused on the possible disappearance of the Republican party. In the tumult of the times, each party's fortunes were storm-tossed, and each in turn faced the danger of being dashed into pieces by a party realignment.

The Concept of Realignment

Just what are party realignments and why are they so important? Historically, observers had always noted changes in party fortunes from election to election, but seldom analyzed those changes in a scientific manner. However, in the 1930's American scholars began to use both European-type sociological hypotheses and individual-level mass interview-type data.[6] These two techniques, in combination, produced a transformation in American political science which led to the effort to create and test theories and models of change. In the voting field scholars began to notice that from time to time elections occur which seem to produce permanent alterations in voting patterns. Such permanent shifts are distinct from the occasional "upsets" which drive out the dominant party because of some short term scandal or setback.

These realigning elections were first identified in clearcut form by V.O. Key, who preferred the term "critical election."[7] According to Key, these elections were characterized by "deeply concerned" voters, by a level of electoral involvement which was "relatively quite high," by "decisive results" which produce "a sharp alteration in the pre-existing cleavage within the electorate" and by an outcome which is "both sharp and durable."[8]

Key was appropriately modest about his observations and called for additional effort to fill in the model. As he had hoped, his effort inspired a generation of scholars and produced many subsequent attempts (one by Key himself) to refine his concept, or to apply it to historical data.[9]

One of the most influential of these efforts was that of Angus Campbell.[10] Campbell, working closely with other scholars at the University of Michigan, developed a more comprehensive typology which included both realigning and non-realigning elections. Campbell's effort was different from that of Key in that it was firmly rooted in the analysis of mass survey data (Key's data had been regional in scope and aggregate in nature).

Focusing on the distinction between party voting and crossover voting on the one hand and shifts in party identification on the other,

14

Campbell detected three major types of election: a maintaining election, in which identifications remain stable and party voting is high; a deviating election in which identifications remain stable but party voting is low; and a realigning election in which party identifications are altered in a permanent way so as to produce a change in the party makeup. Realigning elections of the past, according to Campbell, have been characterized by national crisis, intense voter feeling, a focus on issues rather than personalities, polarization, and perhaps more importantly, a class vote, linked to "compellingly important" economic issues which take an ideological form.

This attempt to discern the root causes of the change rather than to simply focus on the actual vote is an important step which others quickly adopted. Ladd and Hadley, for example, urge scholars to keep in mind that voting is a dependent variable which is the product of other forces. Critical alignments, they sugest, "take place primarily as *effects of* other major changes occuring in the society," changes which are closely linked to "crucial economic transformations" and the emergence of "new social collectives."[11]

The Sundquist Model

One of the most comprehensive efforts to develop a model of alignment-realignment is that of James Sundquist. Sundquist uses a mix of historical and empirical (mostly aggregate) data to develop and test a deductive model. It is an admirable effort which builds upon previous research and conceptualizations to formulate a scientific model which is then subjected to close historical scrutiny and reformulated in light of observed weaknesses. Sundquist's model is much too broad to be totally appropriate to the present study since it is set in historical context and focuses to a large extent upon how parties and leaders respond to conflict over time. However, as a deductive model it has several attractions.

To begin with, it sees as the center of any realignment a tension between old issues (on which the previous alignment was based) and new issues (which are emerging as the basis of a possible new alignment). Such a concept is critical to the present study. Sundquist recognizes that party identities (which in a sense summarize and recapitulate previous conflict patterns) are stable over time and are abandoned only reluctantly. Thus his model focuses on the tension between forces of stability and forces of transformation.

Second, Sunquist recognizes that social-economic changes in society

15

are often pre-conditions of a realignment, but that a political dimension is also necessary. For tensions to become transforming forces they must first be changed into "issues" by political leaders. Thus "alteration in the social, economic, and demographic composition of the society . . . do not in themselves produce realignments. They must first give rise to genuine *political* issues."[12]

This insight by Sundquist is a very valuable one for a study which wishes to use survey data based upon individual responses. Sundquist largely ignores the availability of such data and hence misses an opportunity to test some of his hypotheses from different perspectives.

A third attraction of the Sundquist model is that it distinguishes between dramatic transforming elections (of the type described by Key) and less dramatic "shifts in the party balance," which are often the results of demographic changes of a nonpolitical nature. While recognizing both as important, Sundquist focuses his analysis upon the former. He also singles out the one or two elections when most of the shift occurs, treating only peripherally the followup "aftershocks" which always come after such an earthquake.[13] Since the present study is temporally limited to the period between 1972 and 1976 such a focus is essential.

In actually developing his model of a realignment, Sundquist begins with the assumption of a pre-existing alignment perhaps several generations old. This alignment emerged from a past conflict of some kind which had polarized society sufficiently to alter the party system in a permanent way. As time passed, the dominant mode of opinion on that issue had become widely dispersed throughout society, the balance between the two parties had stabilized, and the issues had faded as party leaders of all types came to grips with the realities of winning elections. The excitement of previous eras waned as new generations did not remember the battles of the past. "Free silver" was as irrelevant to Roosevelt and Hoover as a left-over speech on slavery would have been to Bryan or McKinley.

The new era begins unobtrusively, perhaps with a change in social make-up, a new set of felt needs, an unresolved problem. It is often precipitated by a crisis or problem which will not go away and which becomes politicized. For this issue to realign the parties, three characteristics are necessary: it must be a major issue on which many people have an opinion; it must be a controversial issue which splits the public; and it must be an issue which cuts across the pre-existing alignment instead of reinforcing it. With these qualifications, the new issue is

16

capable of creating a tension within the existing parties, as one or both of them will be internally divided.

This internal division is probably potentially disruptive for both parties, if it is serious enough. Consequently both sets of party leaders will try to straddle or avoid the issue.

Some issues, of course, are so complex and ill-understood that they can be obscured by party centrists. Others cannot. The expansion of slavery, for example,

> was a clear policy question, and one that was simply and easily drama-
> tized. By its very nature, it compelled distinct and opposing positions.
> Slavery had to be either legal or illegal in a given territory; a middle
> position could not be found.[14]

Even if the issue itself is not so compellingly simple, party leaders may simplify it. How to recover from the Great Depression was an extremely complicated issue, but it was brought to the center of the political arena by Hoover's attempts to ignore the problem and Roosevelt's attempts to dramatize it.[15]

If the issue is a persistent one, this effort to avoid a position will fail. Issue-oriented factions within the parties will strive to force the issue, thus accelerating the tension between the old guard and the insurgents. The insurgents will become increasingly disenchanted with the party leadership, and will flirt with allies in the opposition party and with potential third party leaders. Party leaders will intensify appeals to the old loyalties, perhaps convincing some, but never convincing the new-issue enthusiasts.

Sundquist sees several alternative outcomes. It is possible, of course, that both parties will adopt the new issue and hence remove it from the conflict arena. It is more likely that one party will be more subject to issue-activist pressure or will adopt the issue out of tactical concerns (perhaps the minor party, unless it is more divided on that dimension).

If one of the major parties does take a stand, realignment will begin. The realignment will be simple, with no third party playing a major role. This was the case in the Roosevelt 1932 realignment, where the biggest third force was a Socialist Party that could command less than a million votes. If the two major parties delay taking a stand on a re-aligning issue, the partisans of the matter, frustrated by the continued fence-straddling of the two major parties, may move to create a third party. If one of the major parties *then* responds, realignment may occur through the movement of the third party voters into the responsive major party.[16] This happened to the Populists in the 1890's, as they were absorbed into the Bryan Democratic party. Some of the Republican strategists of our own time, dreaming of a new Republican majority, thought they could reap a harvest of Wallace's American Independent party if Nixon would pursue a "southern strategy" in 1972.[17] If the dominant parties continue to be unresponsive to an emerging third force, one of them may be swept away entirely and replaced by the third party. Such a process gave birth to the Republican party in the 1850's.[18]

One possibility not envisioned by Sundquist is that the issue will persist at a secondary level, rising and falling in salience from election to election, without producing a realignment or a resolution, but creating an on-going disruption and instability. This is a possibility which will be examined further in chapter five.

A point implied earlier is that there seems to be a regular time interval which separates eras of political instability. From 1824 to 1860 is 36 years. From 1860 to 1896 is 36 years. From 1896 to 1932 is 36 years. Like the eruptions of America's Old Faithful geyser, the American party system has been disrupted and realigned with a slightly irregular periodicity. This three or four decade cycle may be simply due to chance. A possible explanation, however, and one relevant to the contemporary American scene, is the way in which issues seem to go through a life cycle of their own. Much of this cycle is tied to the acquisition of political values by the young. Party identification is to a very large extent inherited.[19] We acquire it from our parents along with our last name and our religion. But there are pressures on the young to break them away from their party identity. Pressure from peers, colleagues, spouses, and neighbors all put a certain stress on individuals. To the young, the battles of the past are ancient history. The logic which led one's father to become a Democrat or a Republican or a Whig belongs to a former era. The farther one gets in time from the origins of that era, the more weakened are the attachments to it. After two generations (say, 35 or 40 years), the response of children and grandchildren to the clarions of the past are almost negligible. New concerns, new interests, new values, and new goals become predominant in the thinking of the contemporary generation. While it is possible for massive shifts of adult voters to occur, far more often it is the young who move *en masse* in one direction and thus build into the party of their choice a near-invincible margin of victory which will last until they are, in turn, pushed aside by some successive generation. For example, between 1932 and 1936, most first-time voters were becoming Democrats. By and large these first-time voters remained in the party and remain in it today. The weakness of the New Deal coalition in the 1970's lies not only in the occasional tendency of the old guard to abandon the faith but in the inability of these aging troops to persuade their children and grandchildren of the justice of their cause.

Thus, there are two critical components of each realignment: new issues which shatter the faith of the faithful, and the process of aging, death and generational change, which replaces the old faithful with uncommitted voters. The 30 or 40 year interval is not built in. It could be 20 years or 60 years, according to circumstances. What is built in is that after 30 or 40 years, a certain stress or weakness begins to emerge in the old alignment. It may continue to win elections, but sooner or later its vulnerability becomes obvious. Then, given the right issues and the right set of conditions, it will emerge a triumphant and revitalized behemoth, disappear entirely, or find itself a tattered and beaten fragment of its past, condemned to decades of second-place finishes and unproductive opposition, for in the words of Samuel Lubell,

> Our political solar system . . . has been characterized not by two equally competing suns, but by a sun and a moon. It is within the majority party that the issues of any particular period are fought out; while the minority party shines in reflected radiance of the heat thus generated.[20]

Party Systems of the Past

According to Sundquist, a realignment can take one of three forms. In a simple realignment, the former majority party sinks to minority status, while the minority party rises to primacy. In a complex realignment, one of the two major parties is wiped out altogether and replaced by a third party. In a converting realignment, many voters change party identification, but because voters shift in both directions, no change in the majority and minority status of the parties occurs. The majority party remains in the majority, but the popular base of each party is significantly new.

Since the advent of universal male suffrage in the 1820's only three basic realignments have occurred: in the 1850's, in the 1890's, and in the 1930's.[21] The 1930's was a simple realignment (the Democrats became the majority party; the Republicans became the minority party), the 1850's was a complex realignment (the Whigs disappeared and were replaced by the Republicans), and the 1890's was a converting realignment (Republicans remained the majority party but with a new and increased support base). The history of these changes will reveal much about what an alignment is and how it can be transformed.

The modern American two-party system was born in the era of Andrew Jackson with the adoption of universal male suffrage. In the first years, the system revolved around the struggles for power between the dominant Democratic party and the rival Whig party.[22] While the parties did alternate in power, the Democrats controlled the White House and Congress most of the time. The key issues which divided the parties involved the role the federal government would play in the development of the West. The basic social division was the Anglo-American against the Irish, Scottish, and German immigrants. These ethnic divisions bred disputes between the parties on life-style issues such as Sunday "blue laws." As for rivalries between North and South, these had been defused by the Missouri Compromise of 1820. The lessening of the sectional rivalry allowed both parties to be genuinely national, with supporters in both North and South.

The party system was fractured, however, by the Kansas-Nebraska Bill of 1854.[23] By allowing the voters of a territory to decide by "popular sovereignty" whether to create a free state or a slave state, it repealed the Missouri Compromise (which had prohibited slavery north of 36°30') and reopened the conflict between North and South. "Bleeding Kansas" erupted into violence as partisans of both sides invaded the state to influence its vote on the slave issue. The Republican party was formed in February, 1854, to protest this expansion of slavery and immediately won millions of adherents with its planks for free land and against the expansion of slavery. The Democratic party was staggered in the elections in the North in 1854, and sustained the greatest loss of strength in the U.S. House of Representatives in the entire 150-year history of the American party system. A series of episodes continued to inflame the sectional conflict. The near-fatal caning of Senator Sumner by Congressman "Bully" Brooks of South Carolina, after Sumner's anti-Southern speech on Kansas, created an image of Southerners as brutal savages. With the Dred Scott decision of 1857 and John Brown's raid on Harper's Ferry in 1859, sectionalism became the dominant cleavage in American politics. The Republican party—appealing primarily to the North and Midwest—did well. The Whigs and Democrats broke into northern and southern factions, with many of their northern adherents supporting Lincoln in 1860. Lincoln became the first president elected without carrying a single southern electoral vote. The Whig Party disappeared, to be replaced by the Republicans in the north, and rendered irrelevant by the secession in the south.

20

This second party system lasted from the 1850's until the 1890's and was the most competitive of all the party systems to date. Until 1874, the Republicans held a temporary majority position because of the election of Republicans in the south by black voters during Reconstruction. But with the withdrawal of northern troops from the south and the disenfranchisement of the blacks, the south returned to the Democratic fold, and an era of even balance between sectional parties persisted on the national level into the 1890's.

At that time, a second major American realignment occurred, as William Jennings Bryan's campaigns on behalf of the farmer superimposed an urban-rural cleavage on the north-south cleavage that had been dominant since the Civil War.[24] Bryan waged a campaign in support of the working man in 1896 and again in 1900. But his efforts to create a coalition of farmers and urban workers failed. The nativist, agrarian radicalism of his free-silver campaigns frightened many urban voters into the Republican party, and the conflict between Catholics and Protestants in the cities split the labor vote into Democratic and Republican camps.[25] The Republicans emerged from these campaigns as the dominant party down to 1932. In this 40 years of Republican rule, only one Democratic president—Woodrow Wilson—was elected, and he won only because the Bull Moose revolt of Teddy Roosevelt split the Republican ranks in 1912. The critical importance of realignments is driven home by the fact that Bryan, by driving urban voters into the Republican camp, delayed Democratic party hegemony for four decades.

The Great Depression of the 1930's was, of course, the force that ended this Republican era. The inability of the Hoover administration to inspire confidence in its approach to economic recovery, the popularity of Franklin Roosevelt's New Deal, and the decision of the Republicans to run on an anti-New Deal platform in the 1936 presidential campaign all contributed to this third realignment.[26] The period from 1932 to the end of the 1970's is the era of the modern American party system. It was an era of clear Democratic dominance. The Republicans elected only two presidents. One, Eisenhower, was a war hero who almost became a Democrat. The other, Nixon, was elected to his first term with a mere 44% of the vote.

By 1972 this era seemed at an end. In the 1930's Franklin Roosevelt had united a powerful Democratic Party by calling for the regulation of big industries and social welfare programs to help the poor. His programs, such as social security, TVA, and regulatory agencies, were controversial in his day, but as the years passed became less so. Most

21

Republicans came to accept them. Many observers felt that the old issues which had won Roosevelt such striking victories were no longer meaningful to the average voter. New issues had emerged which split the parties, especially the Democratic party, in a new way.

The Roosevelt majority had been built upon the working class, the cities, the ethnic and other minorities, and the south. In many people's thinking, the changes of the 1950's and 1960's had undermined this alliance. Under particular assault was its hold on southern voters and on northern white metropolitan voters. The increasing prosperity of working class people in America and the movement of many workers to the suburbs (where they enjoyed a suburban life style and a middle class identity) in some ways made the workers of America more logically Republican than Democratic. Likewise the immigrant population of America had, over two or three generations, been assimilated and were no longer considered "outsiders." Now, on the contrary, they sometimes seemed to take the opposite side, condemning those still in the cycle of poverty, and those who espoused "un-American" positions or unconventional life-styles. Many people think that this "growing up" of some of America's oppressed social and economic groups will ultimately deprive the Democratic party of its majority and initiate a major party realignment.[27]

Is Realignment Underway, or Is This an Age of De-alignment?

Most observers—scholars and pundits alike—are in agreement that the New Deal coalition, which dominated the American electoral scene for four decades, was by the 1970's a weakened shadow of its former self. Elections in 1952, 1956, 1968, and 1972 showed major defections from the coalition. Groups which were particularly likely to defect were southerners, urban Catholics, and workers.[28] Opinion polls showed decreasing levels of identification with "liberalism", a bad sign for the liberal Democratic party.[29] At the same time, polls showed an increasing level of concern about issues which cut across the Democratic-Republican spectrum. In particular, the social issue and individual candidate qualities seemed to motivate voters more than in past elections. All these factors fit the model of realignment.

On the other hand, the polls did not show any fundamental shift in party balance where identification was concerned. While attachment to parties has decreased over the decade, there was no evidence that the Republicans were gaining adherents. On the contrary, the northern WASPs, the largest support group for the Republican party, were moving toward independent status in the same way as the support groups of the Democratic party.[30]

As Ladd and Hadley point out, for the first time the decay of an old alignment is occurring in an anti-party age; therefore, instead of re-alignment, we may see another kind of transformation of the party system.[31] In the new system, which we can already begin to see around us, voter attachment to both parties will be weakened; majorities will be more volatile over time; presidential voting will be dissociated to some extent from subpresidential voting; and the mass media will take over many of the communications functions handled in the past by political parties.[32] The impact of these changes on the democratic process is not clear. Surely the weakening of the parties represents a step away from the "responsible two-party government" model which a generation of political scientists idealized.[33] Ladd and Hadley take a more optimistic view:

> The contemporary party system displays this dimension: nominee-oriented, issue-directed, media-utilizing, and media-assessed candidacies operating within the formal structure of political parties. We see no reason to lament this development. An electorate which engages with abandon in ticket splitting is much more volatile than one marked by party regularity, but does not seem inherently less capable of effective democratic participation. It will indeed violate the political interests of some to see increasingly porous parties ever more susceptible to take-overs by successive waves of issue activists; but this involves the democratic power struggle, not a crisis of democracy.[34]

The Role of Leadership

It has become commonplace to say that citizens vote on the basis of either party loyalty, positions on the issues, or personal qualities of the candidates. But the third of these has been of the least interest to political scientists. The realignment theory we have described tends to de-emphasize candidate qualities and to focus instead on party loyalties and issues. Such a focus is quite valuable, but decades of research have shown that some voters prefer a candidate not because the candidate is close to them on the issues or of the same party, but because the candidate seems to have attractive personal or leadership traits. Unfortunately, the major voting studies have de-emphasized this fact. As a result, voter concern for candidate qualities has been reduced, both conceptually and empirically, to a residual role. Conceptually, a concern for such qualities has often been explained in terms of low

23

voter information levels (an empirically verifiable observation, at least in the past). Empirically, the study of such traits has often relied upon open-ended questions which are not as precise as one would wish.[35]

In the present study we have developed several measures which we feel will help overcome this deficit. These are listed in Table 1.1. In studying these traits, we are not necessarily suggesting that they are the most important criteria on which to evaluate presidential candidates.[36] Nor are we suggesting that they are a comprehensive list. For example, in a highly institutional system such as that found in the United States, an ability to work with congress (not in our study) is probably more important than a candidate's intelligence. Likewise, many traits which are valuable for getting elected (a clear-cut moral position on a controversial issue, for example) may be counter-productive for the office holder.

In choosing these questions we have singled out certain items which seem to receive media attention (and presumably voter attention) during campaigns, especially recent campaigns. We chose these through a monitoring of news reports, pre-testing, comments from respondents on open-ended questions, and previous studies.

We have also kept in mind two findings of social psychologists who have studied leadership patterns: First, leadership traits are not simply the qualities of "great men." They are those virtues perceived by the voters and produced out of an interaction between the qualities of the candidates, the political culture of the community, and the events and issues that become salient in the campaign. Second, because events do matter, and because some elections seem to produce a candidate who deviates very far from the norm on a trait, and thus focuses great attention on it, the relative importance of the traits will vary from one election to the next.[37] But the importance of candidate traits in presidential elections is one sign of a party system disintegrating rather than realigning (see chapter five).

The City of Dearborn

To study the new public mood and its political consequences, we focused our attention for three years on Dearborn, Michigan, a northern suburban community of just under 100,000 people. We drew a sample of 801 people from this community for interviewing and reinterviewing on four separate occasions. The four waves of interviews were done in February–March 1974, February–March 1975, Febru-

TABLE 1.1
Items used to measure voter perception of personal traits important to presidential candidates.

A. Abilities on specific issues
    1. Capable of managing the economy
    2. Capable of keeping down taxes and the cost of government
    3. Able to keep the peace
B. General talents, useful on all issues
    1. Related to a specific presidential role
        a. a good moral example (role as head of state)
        b. concerned about the public (role as an elected official)
        c. honest in dealings with the public (role as an elected official)
    2. Not related to a specific role
        a. strong
        b. experienced
        c. inspiring
        d. reasonable
        e. intelligent

---

ary–March 1976, and November 1976. The questions asked are in the back of the book along with the dates when each question was asked and a discussion of the sampling procedure.

Dearborn is typical of many older suburban communities. Almost entirely white, it shows the remnants of past immigration waves. Twelve percent of the population is foreign-born and report one or more parents of foreign birth. Most of these immigrants came from the British Isles, Canada, Ireland, and German-speaking Western Europe. Three distinct 'ethnic' blocs exist in the city, however. These are Poles, Italians, and Arabs. Poles and Italians represent 30% of the townspeople with parents born overseas. The impact of these people on the churches, social institutions, cultural interests, and politics of the community is considerable. Dearborn's 'new' ethnics are the Arabs. Five percent or more of the city's population may be Arabic speaking, though many are temporary residents who either move to better jobs or sometimes return to their homelands after a short while. In any case, the Arabs live mostly in the south-end neighborhood of Salina beyond the giant Ford Motor Company Rouge Plant, are less visible and active outside of their neighborhood and have yet to become full participants in the political system.

One unusual characteristic of Dearborn is its collective advanced age. Its median age of 36 years is ten years older than many comparable communities in the area because, while most of the suburban communities underwent population explosions in the 1950's and 1960's, Dearborn was booming in the 1930's and 1940's. Between 1940 and

1950, for example, its population increased from 63,000 to 95,000. Many of these residents remained and are still living there. Movement out of the community is relatively uncommon and housing turnover rates are exceptionally low. This means that, as young Dearbornites come of age, they are not able to find housing within the community. Each school graduation sees a rise in the average age of the community, a decline in the number of people living in each house, and a fall in school enrollments.

This trend has been accentuated by the determination of the city government to encourage single family dwellings and to discourage apartment buildings and other multiple-family dwellings. With the amount of available land almost exhausted, the number of new homes constructed is very small. From 1960 to 1970, a time of booming construction in much of the suburban areas surrounding Detroit, Dearborn households increased by a mere 2.1%. But people seem to like Dearborn: not only do few homes go onto the housing market, but when they do, they sell at a faster rate than in most other communities in the metropolitan area. New construction picked up after 1970 as the Ford Company opened up large tracts of choice, vacant land for housing and condominium construction.

In terms of income, Dearborn is prosperous but not affluent. Much of its population is employed at Ford and the smaller industrial enterprises located within the city. Both management and labor are well represented within the population. While the community was hard hit by seasonal unemployment and the recession of 1974, it was cushioned somewhat by state unemployment benefits and contractual subsidies and supplements for the unemployed. In 1970, the average family income of $12,600 (mean) was 8% less than neighboring Dearborn Heights, a community still undergoing growth and boom, but was 40% more than Detroit. Looking at the bottom of the economic scale, Dearborn had only 3.9% of its families below the poverty level, versus 11.3% in Detroit, and only 1.7% receiving public assistance, versus 8.3% in Detroit.

In terms of family structure and family stability, Dearborn again appears to be well off. Ninety percent of all children under the age of 18 are living with two parents, divorce rates are relatively low, and less than 3% of all families have a female head.

In short, Dearborn is a city which is well established if not well-to-do, which is oriented to the home at a time when family ties seem to be under a strain, which is white and to a certain extent white ethnic, which seldom sees poverty or untreated disease, and which is protected from, though not invulnerable to, the ebb and flow of economic disruption.

Outside forces, however, buffet Dearborn and threaten its stability. Specializing as it does in the manufacture of consumer durables, it is especially prone to high unemployment during nationwide recessions. In the middle 1970's, its standard of living was damaged by inflation.

The most threatening outside force, however, comes from neighboring Detroit, which has one of the highest crime rates in the nation. During the years of our study, its murder rate per person was equal to that in war-torn Belfast. Dearborn protrudes into and is enclosed on two sides by Detroit, and Dearbornites spend many hours discussing the rising tide of violence there. As a consequence many of the residents of Dearborn refuse to travel into Detroit, and the metropolitan area has lost any sense of community it may once have had.

Dearborn was an appropriate site to conduct a panel study for a number of reasons. First, as will be seen in the next chapter, opinions in the community are fairly typical of northern urban whites. Second, by class, by ethnicity, by race, and by religion, many residents are typical of those white lower and middle class ethnics at whom Richard Nixon directed his New Majority appeals. In the early 1970's Dearborn was a community on the periphery of a high crime area and was threatened with court-ordered, cross-district busing. It was also 45% Catholic, a group which has been suggested as a potential major source of Republican recruits.[38]

A final reason for Dearborn's appropriateness was its low rate of geographic mobility, which made it possible to reinterview the same people year after year. City Hall records indicate that less than 3% of Dearborn dwelling units had new occupants during fiscal 1973–1974, and three quarters of the residents lived in the same house from 1965 to 1970.

A study of Dearborn does present some problems, however. It is a community with many older people. In our sample of heads of household, the age patterns were as follows:

AGE	PERCENT
30 and under	13
31–40	18
41–50	21
51–60	22
61–70	15
over 70	10

In short, we are dealing with heads of houseold in an older community. If political change is occurring in the United States only because old people with old ideas die and are replaced by young people with new ideas, then we will miss the change. If, on the other hand, political change is occurring (either in a realigning or converting fashion) because of learning and change in already active voters, then a community like Dearborn, with strong cross-pressures, should reflect these changes.

CHAPTER 2: We Hold These Truths Self-Evident

It is a very risky business trying to draw generalizations about what groups of people believe, but that is the goal of this chapter. Beliefs and values are held by individuals, and each individual has his or her own motives and logic and reasons for believing a certain way. Likewise, when we do study group patterns, we find that there are vast differences by age, class, generation, education, religion, ideology, and a host of other factors. But with these cautions and reservations stated, we would like to argue that there are certain perspectives or views which are so widespread in society that we can conclude that they do somehow constitute a community value system. We will try to outline this community value system in a coherent manner so that in subsequent chapters we can show the impact which it has in different circumstances.

Likes and Dislikes

We started our analysis of Dearborn public opinion with an assumption: to understand a community one should examine its loves and its hates. The instrument that aided our exploration is called a feeling thermometer.[1] We use this device in the field by showing respondents a picture of a thermometer and saying:

> There are many groups in America that try to get the government or the American people to see things more their way. We would like to get your feelings towards some of these groups.

> We have here a card on which there is something that looks like a thermometer. We call it a 'feeling thermometer' because it measures your feelings towards groups . . .
>
> If you don't know too much about a group, or don't feel particularly warm or cold towards them, then you should place them in the middle, at the 50° mark.
>
> If you have a warm feeling toward a group, or feel favorably toward it, you would give it a score somewhere between 50° and 100°, depending on how warm your feeling is toward the group.
>
> On the other hand, if you don't feel very favorably toward some of these groups—if there are some you don't care for too much—then you would place them somewhere between 0° and 50°.

Using this approach, we learned people's loves and hates, first about groups, then about individual political leaders.

The pattern which emerges from Dearborn is typical of northern white America. In fact, when we compare Dearborn with the results of a national survey obtained two years earlier, the pattern is not much different (see Table 2.1).

In Dearborn, the warmest feeling of all is expressed towards the police, followed by young people and whites. Teachers, Protestants, and Catholics receive the next warmest responses. The military, Democrats, and Jews are placed slightly lower but still positive. Labor unions and big business are tied in the next position down, followed closely by blacks. Conservatives slightly outscore liberals to take the next position. Republicans follow, barely above the 50° mark. Women's liberation and politicians fall in the cool area below 50°. Then, much further down come homosexuals, marijuana users, black militants and urban rioters, whose overall scores are so low that they constitute definite "out groups" with no recognizable bloc of supporters.

Among the political figures ranked (and remember that the data reported in this table are from the 1974 wave, at the height of the Watergate crisis) the highest score is for Gerald Ford, at the time still vice-president. He receives about the same score as big business, labor unions, and blacks. Senator Sam Ervin of the Watergate investigation ranks second, followed closely by Governor George Wallace and Governor Ronald Reagan. Senator Edward Kennedy is barely above 50°, while Senator George McGovern falls below that mark into the cool category. Next comes President Nixon, who had not yet been indicted by the House Judiciary Committee but who was under daily attack in

TABLE 2.1
*Thermometer Scores**

Group	SRC 1972 National Study	Dearborn
Police	75	80
Young people	78	79
Whites	77	76
Teachers	—	72
Protestants	74	72
Catholics	67	68
The military	70	66
Democrats	66	66
Jews	66	65
Labor unions	56	61
Big business	53	61
Blacks	64	60
Conservatives	61	58
Liberals	54	54
Republicans	63	52
Women's lib	46	49
Politicians	—	45
Homosexuals	—	31
Marijuana users	21	25
Black militants	17	21
Urban rioters	12	13

POLITICAL LEADER

Gerald Ford	—	62
Sam Ervin	—	58
George Wallace	49	57
Ronald Reagan	—	55
Edward Kennedy	55	53
George McGovern	49	47
Richard Nixon	65	41
Spiro Agnew	54	28

*Italicized items indicate a statistically significant difference between Dearborn and the Nation (at the .01 probability level), using the Standard Error of the Difference Between Means.

the media. At the bottom of the list is former Vice-President Spiro Agnew, fallen to the level of homosexuals and marijuana users after pleading no contest to felony charges. In short, politicians do not receive high marks. The highest ranking goes to the newly appointed vice-president (Ford), a politician with no prior voter recognition, and the second highest to a righteous purger of corrupt politicians (Senator Ervin), who was performing a quasi-judicial function at the time.

31

Dearborn Compared to the Nation

Dearborn responses are very similar to national patterns two years earlier. Some noteworthy differences do appear, however. Conservatives and Republicans are less well liked and George Wallace is noticeably more well liked. Wallace had long been a favorite in Dearborn, and the Republicans, by 1974, had fallen on hard times. Unions and big businesses both seem to have higher esteem than in the nation as a whole, perhaps a reflection of the relative industrial wealth in the town, and of the fact that both union and management are well represented in the sample. One must also keep in mind that the Ford Company has been generous in the past to the community (in the tradition of Henry Ford). It built a spacious library in honor of Henry Ford's 100th birthday and contributed to many other public projects. While Dearborn was the center of violent labor-management clashes in the past, these events are at least a generation away. The 1950's and the 1960's saw a period of remarkable industrial prosperity interrupted only by occasional economic downturns. If we compare attitudes to big business with attitudes to labor unions we find that a full 58% of all respondents view both labor and management in positive terms. While there are some people who see a fundamental conflict between labor and management, the intense antagonism of the past seems to have abated in the eyes of most of our respondents.

We conclude that the likes and dislikes are not much different from overall national patterns. Near the top of the list are police, young people, teachers, and the military, all representing in one way or another a conventional view of society, value transmitters, value defenders, or value receptors.

Looking at the negative end of the scale, we see urban rioters, marijuana users, homosexuals, politicians, and women's liberation—an unsavory collection in the eyes of most respondents. In general, these groups seem most opposed to conventional values. Rioters, we suspect, would receive a negative rating among any population since they seem to overtly challenge others. But some of the other groups make no overt challenge to anything. Homosexuals and marijuana users, for example, are generally unobtrusive in their practices. Even so, our respondents seem to single them out for opprobrium.

Where parties and ideologies are concerned, we find Democrats noticeably higher than Republicans, but conservatives slightly above liberals. The Democratic-Republican pattern is not surprising, considering that the sample is about 2–1 Democrat (approximately the same as that found in national samples). It is interesting that politicians are so low on the popularity scale. National polls have of course shown a declining trust in politics over the past decade.[2] Other measures which we have of political alienation and distrust (discussed later in the chapter) reflect a somewhat more mixed pattern, with some evidence of alienation, but other indications of trust.

Generational Value Systems

We have seen what the public thinks about other groups and about national leaders. But what are they themselves like? What are the basic values of these people, how did they get these values?

In a nutshell, we find them to be happy, guardedly optimistic, wealthy, and materialist in a way characteristic of an older generation of people in the United States and Europe. A few years ago, Ronald Inglehart suggested that the generation gap was emerging as a new political cleavage in the Western world.[3] This cleavage pitted the "new politics" of Eugene McCarthy and George McGovern against the "old politics" of Mayor Daley and George Meany. While it is hardly original to point to the generation gap in an era of student protest and demonstrations against those "over 30," Inglehart was original in arguing that the new cleavage had its roots in the elemental units of human motivation, and that it would persist and bring about fundamental value change over the decades as a result.

Inglehart believed that the young were motivated by fundamentally different, higher psychological needs than their parents. The logic behind this strong assertion lay in the work of Abraham Maslow, who had proposed that human needs are arranged in a hierarchial fashion.[4] The hierarchy begins with the lowest, physiological needs. These are the needs for food, water, air, and sex. "If the physiological needs are well gratified, there then emerges a new set of needs, which we may categorize roughly as the safety needs (security; stability; dependency; protection; freedom from fear, from anxiety and chaos; need for structure, order, law and limits)."[5] Next on the hierarchy is the need for love and belonging. When all these needs are satisfied, a fourth level of need, the need for esteem, emerges: "All people in our society (with a few pathological exceptions) have a need for a stable, firmly based, usually high evaluation of themselves, for self-respect, or self-esteem, and for the esteem of others."[6] Finally, at a still higher rung, when all lower needs are met, emerges the need for "self-actualization," which we might define as the freedom to fully develop as a

33

human, including the right to explore self and society without bond or impediment.

Where an individual fits on the need hierarchy depends upon the experience of adolescence. Deprivation of some basic need during that critical period of value formation will orient an individual throughout life to the pursuit of that goal. Likewise, satisfaction of some need throughout adolescence will liberate the individual from a concern for that goal and will orient him to the next higher unmet need on the hierarchy. If this assumption is true, then children growing up during the Depression or the Second World War will continue throughout their lives to be overly concerned with national security and economic safety. Inglehart refers to such a value system as Materialist or Bourgeois, terms which we will use interchangeably. Likewise, children who grew up in the post-war era of peace and affluence have always lived in an era when their lower needs for economic security and material gratification were met. They as a group would be more oriented to higher needs such as the need for love and belonging, self-esteem and self-respect, or finally self-actualization. John Adams realized the importance of these successive value changes upon societies when he made his famous observation: "I must study war . . . that my sons may study geography . . . in order to give their children the right to study painting."[7]

Inglehart proposes measuring these needs by a question which asks people to name their goals for the nation. Four possible goals are offered. Material—i.e., lower—needs are reflected in "fighting rising prices" and "maintaining order in the nation" as the most important goals. Higher, less materialistic, needs are reflected in a preference for "protecting freedom of speech" and "giving the people more say in important political decisions."* In a second question, Inglehart proposes to measure the material needs with an expression of greater concern for "the fight against crime" and "maintaining a stable economy" rather than "moving toward a friendlier, less impersonal society" and "moving toward a society where ideas are more important than money."*

These measures have been associated with some dramatic behavior patterns. For example, the materialists voted so overwhelmingly for Nixon and the post-materialists so overwhelmingly for McGovern that Inglehart's questions are almost as good as party identification as a predictor of the vote in the 1972 election.[8]

*The first question is subsequently referred to as the First Set or Post-bourgeois; the second question will be called Second Set or Self-Actualization.

The pattern we find in Dearborn is essentially materialist. The maintenance of order is twice as important in the eyes of our respondents as any other item in the first set (see Table 2.2). In the second set, the maintenance of a stable economy and the fight against crime in combination receive 74% of all mentions (see Table 2.3). A true materialist, when faced with two materialist and two non-materialist goals, will rank the materialist goals one-two. This happened frequently in our study. In our first question, 31% of all responders ranked non-materialist goals one and two. In our second question, a full 50% chose purely materialist goals (maintain economy and fight crime) as their first two preferences, while only 9% gave priority to both non-materialist goals.

One of the key ideas to emerge from Inglehart's research is the proposition that there should be large age differences regarding value systems, with the young being much less materialist in an age of increasing prosperity and peace. In fact (as Table 2.4 shows), we did find this to be the case. The young people in our sample are noticeably more likely to have post-materialist values while older respondents are more oriented to economic and security needs.*[9]

Going hand in hand with the presence of a materialist value system is the remarkable level of personal happiness which Dearbornites have.[10] In our three years of research we asked several questions which attempted to measure that satisfaction level and have found it to be consistently high. Dearbornites are, regardless of personal wealth, very happy with their lives.

The specific measure used to tap this attitude was the "self-anchoring ladder," a technique used quite frequently by social scientists.[11] Respondents are shown a ladder with ten rungs on it. They are asked to imagine people standing on this ladder with the most happy people on rung ten and the least happy on rung one. Where would they place themselves?

In response to this, 26% put themselves on the top rung; only 13% put themselves at 5 or below. The average position on this is 7.8 in 1974.

In many ways, Dearborn does have reason to be happy. According to census figures, family income is above average (32% greater family

*This finding of a materialist culture is possibly more dramatic because of our sample's focus on heads of household. This sampling approach overrepresented older residents. Had we more equitably represented younger generation thinking, the percent in the non-materialist category might have increased proportionately, as they have done in the national samples.

TABLE 2.2
Most important goals for the nation (first set)

Maintain order in the nation (Materialist)	42%
Fight rising prices (Materialist)	20%
Protect freedom of speech (Post-Materialist)	20%
Give the people more say in important decisions (Post-Materialist)	17%

TABLE 2.3
Most important goals for the nation (second set)

Maintain a stable economy (Materialist)	42%
The fight against crime (Materialist)	32%
Move toward a society where ideas are more important than money (Post-Materialist)	16%
Move toward a friendlier, less impersonal society (Post-Materialist)	9%

TABLE 2.4
Post-materialist values, by age group

	Age Group		
	21–30	31–50	51+
Post-Materialist Value System (First Set)	19%	15%	11%
Post-Materialist Value System (Second Set)	17%	10%	6%

X^2 of item 1, p=.02
X^2 of item 2, p=.005

income than Detroit); three quarters of the residents are home owners; taxes are low (local industries pay 65% of all property and school taxes); home life seems inordinately stable (90% of all children under 18 years of age live with two parents, and only 13% of once-married people under 54 years of age have been divorced); the educational level is moderate-to-high (12.2 is the median years of education for people over 25 years of age, and this includes a sizeable older population with a relatively low educational achievement level); poverty is uncommon (3.9% of all families are below the poverty level in 1970; 1.7% of all families receive public assistance). When asked about their life's work or occupation, specifically "if you were able, would you prefer another line of work?" only 18% indicated more than passing dissatisfaction; 75% were happy with their occupation.

The sense of satisfaction plays an important, even critical, role in the community value system. Many people here began poor and achieved relative prosperity after years of hard work. We find them oriented to conventional, establishment, materialist values. The intrusion of problems which seem to threaten their security has caused a defensive reaction, accompanied by a feeling of alienation and disillusionment.

Traditional Values and Alternative Life Styles

During the late 1960's and early 1970's, cultural, religious, and life-style conflicts emerged as significant political issues. Abortion, premarital sex, the breakdown of family values, drugs, the role of women, styles of dress, and pornography all entered the political arena. Politicians scurried around trying to take positions on these issues which would either win them votes or else not hurt them too badly. In some cases, highly vocal and determined interest groups emerged to press their point of view on abortion, women's rights, and sex education.

We found a rich variety of opinion on the ten life-style questions (Table 2.5). Respondents were mostly liberal on four of the items, mostly conservative on two, and polarized on the remaining three.[12] To better illustrate the complexity of these issues, we decided to look at the abortion question more deeply. It is a topic which creates intense differences of opinion and is one which has been greatly politicized.

Dearborn is a community where one would expect to find widespread opposition to abortion and support for right to life. Within the city there are large blocs of very traditional neighborhoods with conservative East European populations. The city is 48% Roman Catholic while many other residents are members of conservative protestant denominations. Also, in 1972 there had been a statewide referendum "to allow abortions under certain conditions" which had been defeated in Dearborn by a 57–43 margin. Despite this, by 1974, 70% of our respondents supported a woman's right to an abortion. Of course, our sample does under-represent non-working females who may well be more opposed to abortion than the males and working females whom we over-represent. To the extent that this is important, we may underestimate the extent of opposition to abortion.

But the figure we did obtain is close to the national average. While national studies vary considerably according to how the matter is approached, Gallup, in 1972, asked a question similar to the one we used and found that 64% of his sample agreed.[13] Of course, since 1972 the Supreme Court has legalized abortions, a decision which produced

37

TABLE 2.5
Traditional values and alternative life styles

Item	Response pattern
Most women are better off working in the home	47% agree
Would vote for a woman for president	75% would
Every woman should have the right to an abortion	70% agree
Sex education should *not* be taught in schools	26% agree
A school should have the right to fire a teacher who lets his hair grow too long	16% agree
Dearborn should ban x-rated films	70% agree
A child should not be allowed to talk back to his parents	48% agree
Women's liberation thermometer (% above 50)	39%
Homosexuals thermometer (% above 50)	11%
Marijuana users thermometer (% above 50)	10%

nationwide increase of support for abortion (and also a nationwide increase in the intensity of opposition to it).

In any case, because of popular interest in the subject we looked at the types of people who support and oppose abortion. Age, church, education, ideology and other variables were analyzed. Our results found little differences on most variables but more sympathy for abortion among people who are younger, and less involved with churches. (Table 2.6). We also found that church attendance was almost as important in determining attitude as type of church attended. We had expected that Catholics would be much more opposed to abortion than Protestants, and this was true to an extent. But when we looked at religion and church attendance simultaneously, a different pattern emerged. Now we see that Catholics are more anti-abortion than Protestants but that Protestants who attend services are more anti-abortion than Catholics who do not. Obviously, both faith and involvement have an impact on this issue. The Catholic church as an institution has taken a stronger official stand against abortion than have most Protestant churches, which tend to be more structurally decentralized and not as ideologically cohesive. But in both cases, firm adherence to the church as an organization as evidenced by attendance seems to sum up what might be called the church position.

Race Relations and Busing

Dearborn is nearly all white. According to Mayor Hubbard in our 1974 interview, there were 14 blacks in the city. A look at the recent history of Dearborn shows that the city has not welcomed blacks. Bordered on the east by Detroit and on the west by Inkster—both

TABLE 2.6
Patterns of support for abortion

Variable analyzed	% pro abortion	X^2 significance
By religion		
Catholics	60	
Protestants	69	.0000
By church attendance		
Attenders	58	
Non-attenders	82	.0000
By age		
21–30	76	
31–50	72	.3180
51+	68	
By religion and church attendance		
Catholics who attend	47	
Catholics who do not attend	76	.001
Protestants who attend	69	
Protestants who do not attend	85	

communities with sizeable black populations—Dearborn is an enclave. It has an ugly history of clashes over housing integration. In the 1950's Mayor Hubbard won a smashing re-election campaign in which a major issue was whether or not to have a public housing project (presumably integrated) then being promoted by the Ford Motor Company and Henry Ford II. In 1964, in a widely publicized incident, a black couple helping move some furniture into an apartment in east Dearborn were mistaken by neighbors for new residents and a riot ensued. According to newspaper reports, neighbors stoned the house for hours while police circled the block to make sure the riot did not spread. While Dearborn realtors' offices prominently display open housing leaflets and signs, Mayor Hubbard always felt free to say, "Anyone can live here, but smart people live where they're wanted."

There is a danger, of course, in mistaking the views of demonstrators and a mayor for the views of a whole community. Demonstrators are not elected, and may not represent anyone but themselves. A mayor is frequently elected because he picks up the garbage on time, sends out birthday cards, or runs the city efficiently. In many cases his position on political issues is relatively unimportant. To avoid these problems, our study attempted to systematically examine the views of Dearbornites on racial issues.

We began our study of attitudes towards blacks with the thermometer questions reported in Table 2.1. The black thermometer score of 59.6° put blacks about midway in a list of 21 other social and political groups included in the study. While falling below Protestants, Catholics, and Jews (71.9°, 67.8°, and 65.4°, respectively), they were above other groups, such as conservatives and liberals (58.3° and 54.1°), and well above the other two thermometer items relevant to the black community, black militants (20.9°) and urban rioters (13.4°). Clearly, most residents view blacks warmly to lukewarmly, and black militants coldly.

We asked an open-ended question on advice to blacks, "Many black persons are interested in getting better jobs and in gaining respect in their communities. What advice would you give them to achieve these goals?" Some responses were very liberal, including one respondent who found the question paternalistic and said he had some advice to whites: "Treat blacks like people instead of blacks." On the other hand some respondents were very conservative, like the man who said, "How can you tell them—they won't listen—they're two steps ahead of me already." We classified the answers in a list, with the more liberal answers at the top:

TABLE 2.7
Advice to Blacks

Type of Advice	Percentage citing it
Organize politically	1
Be proud of their culture	11
Achieve more education	51
Be patient	8
Work Harder	19
Stop rioting; obey the law	9
Other	1

Three other items which measured racial-type matters (perceived causes of black unemployment, attitudes toward interracial marriage, and attitude toward busing) were "close-ended." Here respondents were read four possible answers and were asked which of these came closest to their own position (see Table 2.8). Such questions often evoke protests from respondents who feel that the range of alternatives is not complete. While this is a fair criticism, the items are nevertheless valuable because they force respondents to take a position when they would rather not. The item on causes of black unemployment was particularly of this type. Had the questions been asked in an open-ended manner, there would have been dozens of response patterns. As it was, respondents were forced to put themselves into one of four categories, which in turn revealed two major attitude configurations. Persons who suggest that blacks are less reliable than whites (12%) or

TABLE 2.8
Closed-ended questions on racial issues

Items and Responses	Percent
Support for busing	
Strongly favor	0.2
Favor	7.0
Oppose	27.0
Strongly oppose	65.0
Why is the black unemployment rate twice the white rate?	
Blacks are less reliable than whites	12
Blacks are discriminated against	13
Blacks have less training	49
Blacks are less intelligent	27
Attitude toward interracial marriage	
Morally wrong	17
A personal matter	23
I disapprove but feel it is none of my business	23
A person should think carefully before entering such a marriage	37

that blacks are less intelligent (27%) are implying that black unemployment is the result of inherent unemployability of blacks because of moral and intellectual inferiority. We call this "Personal Blame." A typical comment from such a respondent was, "You can't teach them anything." One person suggested that "most of them don't want to work. They want to go straight to the top." Another said, "It is not necessarily a slowness to learn but there are a great many with low motivation." Several insisted that the black unemployment rate was not significantly higher than the white rate, thus denying that a problem existed.

In the second pattern, those who suggest that black unemployment is the result of discrimination (13%) or poor training (49%) are not blaming blacks themselves for their situation but rather blame social conditions or inequities. We call this "System Blame." One such person observed that "they lack skills because of deliberate educational suppression in the past. They had no chance to prove themselves."

The item on interracial marriage also forces respondents to take a position. The answers are designed to proceed from neutrality to moral indignation. On the one end is the view of the 23% who said that such marriages "are purely a personal matter and I have no objection." Admittedly, one of these was the realtor who had "seen some good looking colored chicks," but most of these responses were from non-prejudiced people. An additional 37% said, "I do not object but feel that a person should think carefully before entering such a marriage." Taking these first two response patterns together, we have a total of 60% of our respondents who have given non-prejudiced responses to this question. At the other end of the scale are the other two response patterns. Twenty-three percent said, "I disapprove but feel that it is none of my business." A frequently given reason for such disapproval was the impact of the marriage on the children. Finally, 17% said, "I feel they are morally wrong," including one respondent who added with indignation, "And they are everybody's business." Another emphasized, "God made things different for a reason."

While a majority of our respondents thus reveal themselves to be non-prejudiced on the marriage and unemployment questions, the people of Dearborn are almost unanimous in their opposition to school busing to achieve racial balance. Ninety-three percent oppose busing, including 65% who are strongly opposed.

The reasons for this opposition vary considerably. On the one extreme is the person who proclaimed himself a "racist bigot" and expressed concern that his name be kept confidential so that there wouldn't be any "Detroit black coming to get me." Another person with strong prejudices added that she had moved out of Detroit to get away from "coloreds," which she identified as the major problem facing the metropolitan area: "I really hate blacks, just hate them." Other respondents were more mixed in their reasoning. Several mentioned the problems of having children commute long distances and parental responsibility to choose good schools for their children ("people move to certain areas because of the schools"). One particularly thoughtful man in his 50's with a teenage child observed: "I don't know about the busing deal. I don't think you can say it's good or bad. It might work in Dearborn Heights but not in Dearborn or vice versa. I can see that this would screw up the kids' after-school activities, and I don't think they should be deprived of participating in athletics, events, or plays. I'm not against the colored though. I've met good and bad. I just don't think it's going to solve the problem. It doesn't make sense to me."

In chapter three we analyze in detail the types of people who support and oppose busing. Suffice it to say at this point that the pattern is not always one of simple racial prejudice but is much more complexly integrated into the value system we have been discussing here.

One final item, while not dealing directly with race relations, is relevant here. A proposed alternative to busing, suggested by both liberals and conservatives, is government grants to ensure all schools, including those in poor neighborhoods, equal funding. We asked respondents, "Would you favor a proposal to have the government give each school an equal amount of money for each child so that the schools would be more equal?" Seventy-two percent agreed with the proposal. One of them, a man in his 30's with four children in school, said, "Yes, the poor people should be able to have quality education, too." The remaining 28% disagreed. Their reasons ranged from the 30-year-old male teacher who said, "I am a teacher and I know that money is not the answer," to the 30-year-old female with infant children who said "no" because, "we'd be going into socialism."

Law and Order

If there is one area in which the community seems united, it is on opposition to crime. Dearborn itself, while it has no serious crime problem, borders Detroit and is very sensitive to the major crime problem of that city. Certain metro area papers and television stations also tend to feature and sensationalize crime stories, so that the Sunday evening local television news is sometimes called "the body count." Crime was a matter which was mentioned time and again as a concern or worry. In all three years of the study, crime emerged as the top metro area problem in the eyes of our respondents. In 1974, for example, 44% thought it was the single most serious problem facing the metropolitan area and 62% placed it among the top three problems in seriousness. It remained a high priority item in subsequent waves of interviewing, shifting by only small percents.[14]

Typical of the comments on this subject were those of an older woman who felt that the major problem in the metropolitan area was "fear of street crime . . . fear of leaving home . . . I have some friends in Detroit and you can't even mail anything to them because of the hippies who live next door." A man with several children observed "crime is ruining Detroit. My family and I won't go to the city anymore." Another person who had listed crime as a major problem commented on guns: "The average person needs protection. I own one myself. But we should register them." A fourth person who was in favor of capital punishment, and who rated police at 100° and the military at 85° said "we need more discipline."

As one can surmise, many people are aggressive proponents of law and order policies (see Table 2.9).[15] As mentioned earlier, police lead the thermometer ratings with an average support score of 79.6°. "They've got a tough job to do" said one booster, who summarized

43

TABLE 2.9
Attitudes toward law and order

Item	% who agree
Judges are too soft on criminals	90
Favor capital punishment	75
Crime is one of top three major problems in the metropolitan area	62
Police should be allowed to search suspicious persons without regard to their rights	55
Crime is the major problem in the metropolitan area	44
Every person has a right to own a gun and not register it	16

the feelings of much of the community. This trust was reflected in a willingness to give police more autonomy in dealing with suspicious persons. One policeman, perhaps anticipating criticism that police would or had abused their discretionary power, asserted that "police are trained to tell when a person is guilty. The way they walk . . . the way they act . . . we can sense it . . . we can tell." And while many people expressed reservations about too much police power ("If they're moderate in how they handle it"), it was the rare person who felt that "police are authoritarian . . . stupid . . . inefficient . . . they violate people's rights."

Where punishment was concerned, most people were in favor of capital punishment and were critical of what seemed a tendency for judges to be too easy on the guilty. Asked about executing criminals for serious offenses, one respondent snapped, "The sooner the better." Most people felt it would serve as a deterrent and would "take care of big crime." Judges themselves were almost unanimously condemned for not being strict enough. The rare defender of the bench was the person who observed that "judges are not at fault. They just judge the facts as brought to them. It is the lawyers who are at fault. They are only interested in winning a case."

To understand this intense concern for crime, we found it helpful to look at the characteristics of people who are more and less "hard" on law and order issues.[16] There are different things which could produce this strong law and order position. It could be, for example, that the people with the most wealth would be those most worried about crime. This possibility is weakened, however, by the common finding that most of the victims of crime are not the wealthier elements of society but the poorer. If this is true, we might suggest an alternative hypothesis, that those most concerned about crime will not be the privileged members of society, but rather its most vulnerable elements: the poor, the old, and those physically closest to high crime areas. (In Dearborn this describes the east, adjacent to Detroit.)

There is, of course, a third possibility—that a hard anti-criminal stance is an aspect of a value system in which criminals are viewed as "deviants." If this is true, then a rigid anti-crime position would not be concentrated in certain economic classes, but would be found in those elements of society most likely to be adherents of that value system— the old, the less educated, and those with a more materialistic value system.[17]

To test these hypotheses, we look in depth at one specific item, that being the matter of police searches of suspicious persons. This is controversial because of its possible constitutional implications. The Bill of Rights protects individuals against unreasonable search, against illegal arrests, and against arbitrary treatments of various kinds. The specific question at hand seems to be whether a policeman should be allowed to "stop and frisk" a person who is not suspected of committing a known crime, but looks as if he might have done something yet unreported, or, perhaps more importantly, might be on his way to commit a crime. Proponents of such action argue that police are trained to judge human behavior and can often tell by a person's appearance whether he is guilty. A bare majority of 55% took this position. On the other hand, opponents suggest that giving the police arbitrary power is not only illegal but unwise, since it will lead to an abuse of individual rights. As one of our respondents—a middle aged engineer—put it, "I don't think anybody should be allowed to take away anybody's rights." Proponents then counter that, without sanctity of property and person from criminal elements, individual rights are a meaningless concept.

Table 2.10 reports a breakdown of attitudes toward police search by age, income, education, value system, and region of town. In interpreting this, the idea that it is the better-off classes of society which are the most anti-crime is not supported. Wealth and education both are inversely related to support for police searches. Much more evidence is provided to suggest that a hard anti-crime position is a function of either actual vulnerability or a value system. To support the vulnerability thesis we note that support for police search is concentrated among the old, the poor, and the less educated. It is not disproportionately found in the eastern sector of town, although one might argue that

TABLE 2.10
Support for police search: patterns of response

Variable compared	% pro search	X^2 significance level
By age		
younger	21	
middle	52	.0000
older	73	
By income		
lower	79	
medium	68	.0000
higher	52	
By education		
lower	63	
medium	65	.0000
higher	38	
Post-materialist value system		
Materialist	65	
Mixed	54	.0002
Post-materialist	35	
By region of town		
East (borders Detroit, higher crime rate)	56	.99
West (far from Detroit, lower crime rate)	54	

given the mobility of criminals and the relatively efficient Dearborn police, the moderately lower crime rate in the western half of town is not sufficient to produce big differences in public opinion.

Strongest support is for the idea that anti-crime attitudes are the result of a value system, or a way of looking at the world. Older people, less educated people, and people with a materialistic value system are noticeably more anti-crime in attitudes. In chapter three we will explore more carefully whether vulnerability or ideology is the most important factor in law and order attitudes. Certainly both play an important role.

The Role of the Federal Government

In the 1930's when Franklin Roosevelt was creating the modern Democratic party, he rallied much of the working urban class to his banner by a series of then revolutionary social welfare programs which filled the gap between the promise and the performance of the private economic system. These programs were not designed to redistribute wealth or to equalize it as much as to equalize opportunity and to create a minimum below which most people would not be allowed to fall. They focused upon providing jobs for the unemployed, minimal social services for the poor, and various forms of assistance for all. Roosevelt also developed policies to regulate the free enterprise system. These included supervising and regulating business practices, creating more progressive tax policies through new corporate, capital gains, inheritance and income taxes, and even promoting government ownership of certain key segments of the economy, such as the Tennessee Valley Authority.

Opinion patterns in Dearborn generally favor social welfare programs but are more reserved about certain aspects of government supervision and regulation.[18] To study people's attitudes on these issues we asked a series of ten questions. These questions were of two types: the first type was a simple disagree-agree item such as "Do you agree or disagree with this statement: The government ought to help people get doctor and hospital care at low cost?" The second type was more elaborate. People were read a brief statement describing two opposite points of view, and then asked to put themselves somewhere on a scale of one to seven in terms of how much they agreed or disagreed with the opposing positions. For example:

"As you know, in our tax system people who earn a lot of money have to pay higher taxes than those who earn less. Some people think that those with higher incomes should pay even more than they do now. Others think that such people already pay enough.

(RESPONDENT IS NOW HANDED THIS CARD)

Rich should pay more		Rich already pay enough
	1 2 3 4 5 6 7	

Suppose the people who want the rich to pay more are at one end of this scale—at point one—and those who think the rich already pay enough are at the other end—at point seven.

Where would you place yourself on this scale, or haven't you thought much about this?"

TABLE 2.11
Attitudes toward federal government activism

Type of question	Item	Percent pro government activism
agree/disagree	Inexpensive health care	82
agree/disagree	Education loans	70
agree/disagree	Help people get jobs	67
agree/disagree	Guarantee good standard of living	61
agree/disagree	Housing loans	60

		Percent*		
		Liberal or pro activist	Middle	Conservative or non activist
7-point scale	Rich pay more taxes	60	23	17
7-point scale	Health care (federal matter than private)	53	17	30
7-point scale	More regulation of industry	31	21	48
7-point scale	Run oil companies	28	16	57
7-point scale	More pollution controls even if it hurts the economy	23	9	68

*Four on the scale is classified as middle; 1–3 and 5–7 are activist or non-activist.

The results (See table 2.11) show that on seven of the ten questions, respondents are supportive of federal activities. Strongest support shows up in those items dealing with provisions of assistance or services. Strongest opposition to government activities are in those areas which deal with direct ownership of industry, or interference with industrial autonomy. Clearly the people of Dearborn want the government to be there when they need it, but they are not at all confident that it can assume the functions of business without causing disruption.

At the top of this support list is backing for inexpensive health care (the question quoted above) with 82% endorsement. Health costs have risen dramatically over the past few years and it is obvious that the people of Dearborn feel some action on this front is warranted. The problem is deciding what that action should be. Item seven asks specifically about "a government insurance plan which would cover all medical and hospital expenses" versus the present system whereby medical expenses are "paid by individuals, and through private insurance like Blue Cross." On this specific proposal the support level remains above 50% and the ratio of supporters to opponents is a high 9 to 5. But the 24% decline (from 82% to 53%) as we go from general to specific shows how difficult it would be to get wide support for a specific proposal.[19] Still, considering that many respondents were covered by private plans, the level of absolute support is notable.

The second highest level of support comes on the question of educational loans ("the government should not feel obliged to give loans to poor students"). Education has always been a vehicle for mobility, a social equalizer. That value system clearly persists in Dearborn. A common reservation was "if they are serious students," but even this qualification did not prevent an agreement with the general principle that the government should help children have equal opportunity.

Close behind this is a belief that "the government in Washington ought to see to it that everybody who wants to work can find a job", with 67% support. Like the health care questions discussed above, this makes no specific suggestions as to how this goal would be achieved— through tax incentives to business or through a direct WPA-type government employment program. It also specifies those who want to work, thus dissociating the program from "welfare loafers" and others who may, in the eyes of respondents, want benefits without work. Most Dearbornites share the sentiments of one respondent who said "It is important that everyone work." Several people linked joblessness to street crime. An occasional critic offered an opinion like, "Anyone who wants a job can find a job—most, anyway."

A more open-ended subject is that which suggests that "the government ought to make sure that all people have a good standard of living." This proposal makes no reference to the needy or the "deserving poor." It seems to include everyone, even those who want a free ride. Even so, it receives the support of 61% of all respondents, including the middle-aged worker who felt, "we are the government. It is our job." If this question is any indication, then "big government" programs such as this are not, in principle, seen as undesirable in and of themselves. But from what we have seen above we would suggest that a specific proposal would arouse greater opposition than the principle itself does.

Many critics object on principle to government equalization programs. One such person, an articulate conservative medical doctor, objected with the observation that "the Bible says 'the poor you will have with you always,' we don't need handouts."

At about the same support level as this "standard of living" question we find an item relating to housing policy: "anyone who can't afford adequate housing should be able to get a loan from the government." Here again we see over 60% agreement. "Someone should help them" is a typical observation. Opponents have mixed reasons but comments

49

such as "why can't they afford it? Aren't they willing to work?" were interspersed with more practical considerations such as "how can they pay back the loan if they can't afford the house in the first place?" While the breadth of this endorsement is impressive, one must again question the depth of it. If a housing proposal costing several billion dollars were to be introduced in the Congress the reaction would be hard to predict. Whether the specifics would reduce the support group by a third, as happens with health care, is not certain. What we do see is a philosophical commitment to equity and opportunity which is widespread in the community.

On the seven-point scales, the most popular item is the progressive tax proposal cited above. Here, 60% of all respondents are on the liberal side, and the ratio of proponents to opponents is 18 to 5. Many comments such as "let them pay their fair share" and "there are too many loopholes" permeate the interviews. The occasional "I already pay enough" was rare. As mentioned earlier, Dearborn residents think of themselves as a favored community. One would expect from them a more conservative response pattern, even though a large proportion are working class people whose incomes are not inordinately above average. In fact what we found was that only 17% were willing to agree that "the rich already pay enough." To the extent that the parties make this an issue in future elections (and it was definitely an issue on which the parties took opposing positions in 1972 and 1976), the Democrats would seem to be on the winning side of the fence.

On the three remaining items (all seven-point scales) support for the federal activist position falls to below one third. These three items and the level of support for them are as follows:

Many people have suggested that some of the economic problems of this country are caused by the unwillingness of the government to regulate business and industry; other people argue that the problem is too much regulation . . . 31% were in favor of more regulation, 48% opposed, for a ratio of 8 to 5 opposed.

Some people have argued that the oil companies are so important to the economy that the government should take them over and run them, of course paying the owners for their property. Other people say that the oil industry should be run by private enterprise . . . 28% in favor of takeover, 57% opposed, for a ratio of 2.1 to 1.0 opposed.

In the past few years the government has required that automobile companies put pollution control devices on their cars. Some people have argued that until the economy gets better, no new regulations should be added. Other people argue that these new regulations are very important and should continue as scheduled . . . 23% in favor of continuation, 68% opposed, for a ratio of 3.0 to 1.0 opposed to continuation.

This last item, on pollution regulation, must be interpreted within the light of the economic peculiarities of Dearborn, though it also has wider implications.[20] Many residents from the town work in the big auto plant located within the city boundaries. The recession of 1974 and 1975 which hit the city so hard left its residents sensitive to any new proposal which might affect the job market. Auto magnates have time and again argued that new pollution control regulations would drive up costs and increase layoffs. These statements receive local coverage and seem to have had an impact. Earlier in the interview respondents had been asked if they would be willing to "pay more taxes to reduce pollution" and 67% had said "yes." Again we see the tension which exists between a general principle and a specific proposal. Any proposal seems to alienate a certain percentage of supporters of the principle and to reduce the ranks of the followers. This is particularly true where personal costs (i.e., job security) might be affected.

A further understanding of responses on these three regulatory issues can be gained by two other questions which we asked. Specifically: "The government is trying to do too many things to help people. The country would be better off if many of these programs were ended," (agree/disagree), and "my impression is that most government agencies are not nearly as efficient as the average private company or business." On the first of these, 66% of our respondents agreed and on the second 86% agreed. These two results are very important if one is to understand attitudes towards federal activities. There runs throughout public thinking a general distrust of distant governments, bureaucracy, regulation, and administrative supervision. Part of this is based on a desire for self-reliance and personal achievement, part of it is based upon a feeling that distant governments are not skilled in understanding and regulating business or social relations, and part of it is based upon a distrust of politicians. This distrust and reservation does not mean opposition to government programs, however. The typical person listened to a Wallace or Ford condemn interference and cheered with honest enthusiasm, but on the same day listened to a Udall or Kennedy propose jobs or health care programs and cheered with equal enthusiasm. Many respondents who renounced government inefficiency had supported each and every one of the New Deal programs listed (top half of Table 2.11).

51

The reason these seemingly contradictory positions can exist within one person is that although people are opposed to inefficiency, corruption and wasted expenditures, they are even more opposed to having the government stand aside and do nothing. When a specific problem exists, or when people need help, they want the government to do what it can. The politician who misreads this and campaigns on a platform of terminating government programs will be defeated. On the other hand, the politician will also lose who advocates more such programs without convincing people that they are needed, that they are well designed and efficient, and that they do not interfere with structures or decisions better left in private hands. The Republican conservative candidate who attacks big government in general will strike a responsive cord, but will be seriously hurt if his Democratic opponent counters with "exactly *which* program do you want to cut?"

Who Supports Federal Programs?

To determine patterns of support and opposition for federal programs we compiled an index made up of the five agree-disagree items reported in Table 2.11. For each item on which the respondent reported support for government action we gave one point, so that a person who supported all five government programs would get a score of five and a person who supported none would get a zero. The result (called the New Deal Index) provides an overall composite measure of support or opposition to government programs.* An individual may agree or disagree with a specific program for idiosyncratic reasons without drastically changing his overall position on the index. To simplify analysis, we have broken the index into two parts, with those supporting three or more programs (74%) going into the "high" category and those supporting two or less (26%) going into "low."

The resultant patterns of support and opposition very closely parallel socio-economic status (see Table 2.12): the poor are more supportive than the rich; those in lower status jobs are more supportive than those in higher status jobs; renters are more supportive than home owners; the less educated are more supportive than the more educated; people

*Distribution on the New Deal Index was as follows:

Points on Index	Percent of Sample
0	4
1	8
2	14
3	20
4	26
5	28

TABLE 2.12
New Deal index: patterns of
support and opposition to
government activism

Variable	% high index*
Income	
higher	42
lower	68
Job status	
higher	50
lower	68
Home owner	
owner	52
renter	64
Union member	
yes	65
no**	49
Education	
high	37
medium	67
low	82
Age	
21–30	54
31–50	51
51+	58
Class self-perception	
working	69
middle	46

*All X^2's statistically significant at .05
level or better except for age.
**Includes non-unionized workers as
well as management, professions, etc.

who think of themselves as in the working class are more supportive than those who put themselves in the middle class; union members are more supportive than non-union members. Clearly the pattern reflects a strong class bias. The commonly held belief that America is emerging as a classless egalitarian society is not substantiated by these data. On the contrary, the data suggest that on this key dimension, class is a very salient factor indeed. The division between the rich and the poor, the upper class and the lower class, the educated and the uneducated is a definite fracture which divides the polity.

From one point of view we see evidence of "self-interest liberalism" in these response patterns. Many people form political opinions within the framework of their own personal wants and needs, rather than because of any ideological preferences which would lead them to given policies or goals. Thus a person who needs a new home would be in favor of easy housing loans. Such a person would appear as a "liberal" on this issue, though he is not a liberal at all, but merely a person who wants to pay a lower mortgage rate. Thus even the very rich can emerge as liberals so long as it suits their economic needs. In the short run, the distinction between ideological liberalism and self-interest liberalism is perhaps not critical. The poor would favor government programs whether because of a sense of immediate personal need or because of a sense of social injustice resulting from class oppression. In the long run, however, the "why" of this pattern is of critical importance. A set of demands based in self-interest will be conciliatory and easily integrated. A similar set of demands rooted in class conflict will be harder to resolve, if they are resolvable at all.

Around the turn of the century, the socialist movement split into two camps because of this very issue of whether the conflict between the working and the upper classes was one of distribution or one of fundamental oppression. One camp (centered in the German and British labor movements) felt that short-term strategic gains such as better working conditions, higher wages, and social reform should be at the heart of the reform movement. Most American liberals and progressives (while not socialists) accepted this argument. The other wing of socialism, under the leadership of Lenin, argued that the conflict was more fundamental than a dispute over wages. Even if all the short-run goals were achieved, he argued, the basic fact that the society is run for the benefit of the few would remain.[21]

We cannot tell from our data how fundamental the conflict between the classes is. We cannot say, for example, the extent to which people would be amenable to a "radical" political assault upon privilege. From what we know personally and from what we saw happen in the 1972 election, we strongly doubt that such a campaign would succeed. What we do know, however, is that the division between the classes is much greater than we expected. The decades of economic boom which America saw has not removed the fact that the upper classes have one point of view and the lower classes have another. Though this division is not likely to presage a revolution, it does suggest a very high level of dissatisfaction with the present system of distribution in America. Even if it is not articulated in class terms, the potential for mobilization along these lines is present.

Before we leave the matter of federal activism, however, one more pattern must be discussed—the matter of age differences. Most national studies show that younger people are far more supportive of social welfare programs than the old.[22] The key exception, of course, is on those programs which relate to elderly people (such as medicare or social security), programs on which the elderly tend to be more liberal. But the general pattern that the young are more liberal is a clearly established national trend. We can only speculate as to why Dearborn does not follow this trend.

One possible explanation lies in the items included in the index. Inexpensive health care and helping people maintain a good standard of living are two matters to which elderly people might well respond positively, especially those on fixed incomes or soon to retire. Other items (buying homes, getting jobs, education loans) would be more relevant to younger or middle aged people. We may well have compiled an index which allows each group to respond to its own needs. Such an explanation would be consistent with the "self-interest" thesis stated above.

A second possibility is that the older generation, socialized into the political system by Franklin Roosevelt and the New Deal, is still loyal to those policies. Social scientists have come increasingly to the conclusion that much behavior and attitudinal preferences can be explained in terms of generational value systems. Inglehart has shown this, as have other scholars.[23] We may well have in Dearborn a group of elderly people who experienced labor strife, the Depression, and unemployment, and who came out of it with a firm commitment to government action, a commitment which perhaps exceeds that which the elderly of other communities show.

The Political System

National studies over the past decade have shown a very definite pattern of political alienation and party disintegration.[24] Noninvolvement has increased; non-voting has increased; suspicion and distrust have increased. To a certain extent these trends are seen in our study, but exceptions are evident. Voter registration is very high, as is voter turnout.* People seem generally well informed. They quite often vote a split ticket, but party identification patterns are very similar to national levels. Patterns of alienation and efficacy are mixed but seem a bit on the distrustful side. To see how these various components of

---

*Ninety percent of our sample claimed to be registered and 86% claimed to have voted in the 1972 presidential election. An effort to confirm registration levels by examining the records of the city clerk showed that in most cases the respondent was in fact registered as claimed. The 86% claiming to have voted in 1972 was above the city-wide level but the city figure would include the very young, students living away and others who would depress the average turnout. Such persons were underrepresented in our sample.

political orientation interact requires a more in-depth look. Let us turn first to the question of general political orientation.

Most of our respondents identify themselves as Democrats or as independents leaning to the Democratic party (see Table 2.13). State Democratic leaders view Dearborn as a community where their candidates can build up leads to offset the more Republican suburbs north of Detroit or the rural areas outstate. Still Dearborn is not inordinately Democratic. The 43% Democratic and 21% Republican figures are almost identical to those found in national polls in the mid-1970's.[25] In terms of its political identifications, Dearborn is very typical of the nation as a whole. Like other Americans our respondents show a definite tendency to vote for candidates of either party in statewide and national races (see Table 2.14). Obviously, respondents do not feel bound to vote the straight ticket. While their party attachments are a major factor in understanding their thinking and behavior, those attachments are not always binding when it comes to elections.

There are two possible explanations for this pattern of cross-party voting, especially among Democrats (who seem to be characterized by it more than Republicans). First, the state Republican party is generally viewed as one of the more progressive in the nation and has been successful in recruiting attractive political moderates to run for state-wide office. Many Democrats have responded to these candidates with their votes.

Second, the Democratic party in recent years has been criss-crossed by fault lines of ideological conflict which have periodically erupted in the form of factional disputes. So long as these conflicts exist within the party, any party nominee is likely to evoke opposition from some element of the party and generate a significant defection rate.

Again looking at Table 2.13, we see some possible evidence of this problem. For example, 47% of all respondents report that they first consider a candidate's position on the issues when deciding how to vote. A further 39% look at the candidate as a person, and only 13% consider the party of the candidate first. Chapter five will show that party identification remains a key predictor of a person's vote although, in this age, independent voting is praised and people are often embarassed to mention party. One young woman who admitted voting on party lines put it this way: "An honest answer is party. Most people will say issues, though." Another respondent said he was mostly guided by an evaluation of the candidate's character because, "You can't believe what they tell you about issues."

Table 2.13 also shows an incongruence between party thermometers

TABLE 2.13
Orientation to the political system

Mean Thermometer scores	
Democrats	65°
Republicans	52°
Conservatives	58°
Liberals	54°
Party Identification	
Democrat	43%
Independent, leaning to Democrat	11%
Independent	17%
Independent, leaning to Republican	11%
Republican	21%
Most important consideration when voting (choice)	
Party label of candidate	13%
Issue position of candidate	47%
Qualifications and character of candidate	39%

TABLE 2.14
Voting patterns

Election	Percent
1972 Presidential election	
Nixon	64
McGovern	29
Other or don't remember	7
1972 Senate race	
Republican incumbent	62
Democratic challenger	37
1972 House race	
Democratic incumbent	89
Republican challenger	8
Other or don't remember	3
1973 Mayoral race	
The Mayor	86
The challenger	14
1974 House race	
Democratic incumbent	87
Republican challenger	13
1974 Governor's race	
Republican incumbent	68
Democratic challenger	32

and party identification levels on one hand and liberal-conservative thermometer scores on the other: people prefer Democrats to Republicans, but also prefer conservatives to liberals. Since 1964, the liberal and conservative directions of the national parties have become increasingly distinct, with the Democratic party retaining its traditional center-left position but the Republican party moving to the right, a move which has cost the Republicans some votes.[26] At the same time, however, the proportion of the population identifying themselves as "conservative" has increased.[27] Nationwide, this has meant that the Republican party has become more and more an ideologically cohesive party of the right with only a small liberal wing, and an increasingly reduced base over its pre-1964 levels. The Democratic party, in contrast, has held onto its conservative wing in terms of party identification but has seen itself increasingly factionalized as liberals and conservatives, both very powerful within the party, fight over the issues and candidates.

To see how this conflict was reflected in Dearborn, we compared a person's party identification with whether that person was self-classified as a liberal or conservative on a seven-point scale. The results were intriguing (see Table 2.15): 21% of the people studied called themselves both Democrats and liberals and 17% were Democrat and conservative, a ratio of 6 to 5. On the other hand, only 6% of the sample were Republican liberals while 33% were Republican conservative, a ratio of 1 to 5. Clearly the Republicans have a dominant wing which is able to dictate policy and candidates (at least to an extent). The Democrats, in spite of the fact that their national leaders are generally to the left, are split in terms of their voters between two big powerful tendencies.

We do not wish to overstate this division, for as we will show in chapter four the term "conservative" has symbolic as well as policy implications. Not everyone who claims to be a "conservative" is of the Ford-Reagan-Goldwater persuasion. Still, symbols are important, and labels are important, especially among those people who identify with those labels and symbols. The potential for disruption is ever present within the Democratic party, as the party has seen—much to its dismay—over the past decade.

Are the Parties Different?

One important factor in shaping how people behave toward the parties is the image which the parties have. Sometimes an image is a

TABLE 2.15
*Party Divisions by ideological
self-classification, total %**

Party Identification	Self-Classification	
	Liberal	Conservative
Democrat	21	17
Independent	11	12
Republican	6	33

*This table omits those respondents who put them-
selves at the middle of the road position on the
liberal/conservative scale. They represent 35% of
the sample.

true reflection of a party's actual intentions or accomplishments, and
sometimes it is a distortion. In any case, it is of great importance.
People base their decisions about the parties not so much on what the
parties are trying to do as on what people *think* they are trying to do.
If a certain party is perceived as being warlike, incompetent, or in the
control of a small faction, people may vote against it even if those
things are not true. If people believe that both parties are identical in
their performance or goals, then party loyalty will drop and defection
rates will rise. To find out how people felt about the parties and their
differences, we asked a series of questions which tapped these attitudes. The first question related to whether or not people felt there
was any difference between the two parties or whether they were the
same on most issues. A full 72% stated that there were important
differences between the parties. Table 2.16 shows how people perceive
these differences. On two issues (war and peace, and efficiency in
government), a majority of people feel that there are no important
differences between the parties. It is interesting, however, that of the
minority who felt there was a difference, the percentage preferring the
Republicans was greater than the percentage preferring the Democrats. These two issues are ones on which Republicans have, in the
past, made big gains. Good government by efficient businessmen
rather than hack politicians has also been a Republican theme in the
past.

The pattern changes, however, on the other two issues. Where economic health and personal self-interest are concerned, the Democrats
emerge with broad support. They outdistance the Republicans by margins of almost two to one on the ability to maintain a stable economy,
and by almost three to one on helping people. Again, these are tradi-

TABLE 2.16
Perceived differences between the parties

Item	Democrats	Republicans	No Difference
Which party is better able to maintain world peace?	17%	25%	59%
Which party is better able to promote prosperity and keep the economy healthy?	47%	21%	32%
Which party is better able in the long run to help people like yourself?	43%	15%	42%
Which party is better able to cut waste and inefficiency in government?	13%	26%	61%

tional Democratic strengths dating back to the time of Herbert Hoover and Franklin Roosevelt. Only on rare occasions (for a few months before the 1972 presidential election for example) have the Republicans been seen as the better managers of the economy.[28]

Traditionally, presidential elections have been dominated by two issues: peace and prosperity. When both of these issues are running in the direction of one party, it gives that party a significant advantage. This was the case in 1956. When the parties split the issues, the elections have usually been close (as happened in 1968 when the public favored the Democrats on the economy but the Republicans on ending the war).[29] If one of these issues is neutralized, we would expect the other to give millions of bonus votes to one of the parties. That would seem to be the case in 1976, with peace not an issue and voters looking to the Democrats to restore prosperity.

Of course, there can be short-term fluctuations on these' issues, which temporarily reverse the positions of the parties. Still, looking at things from a long-range perspective, it seems likely that the stereotypes of the Democrats as the party of war and the Republicans as the party of depression are likely to remain for some time, considerably reinforced by the events of the 1960's and 1970's.

Political Information

The people of Dearborn are generally a well-informed population. The metro area is covered by seven television stations and two large urban newspapers. Dearborn itself has a radio station and four weekly papers which are very competitive. In all, 93% of the people we interviewed subscribe to one or more newspapers or news magazines. The result is a group of people who are well informed on matters of local politics and slightly better than average informed on state and national affairs. For example 96% of our respondents could give the name of the mayor, 92% could name the mayor of Detroit, over 60% could name each of the two United States senators, 90% could name the governor, and 95% could name the vice-president. Forty-two % could name their congressional representative. There were other, more obscure, questions people could not answer (only 29% could name the United States Chief Justice) but these were included in the questionnaire specifically to identify the best informed elements of the population rather than to test "average" information.

Alienation, Trust, and Efficacy

There has been a steady increase in alienation levels in the United States since the mid-1960's.[30] People feel that their leaders are unresponsive and dishonest, that the political system is not being run in the public interest, and that they are personally impotent before the vast machinery of society and government. Dimensions of alienation are sometimes called trust and efficacy. Trust is related to an individual's feelings about the political system and the people who inhabit its major posts. Are these people honest? Do they care what people think? Are they more responsive to private interests than public interests?

Efficacy, on the other hand, is a function of the person's own sense of personal influence, regardless of how politicians behave. Do I understand what is going on? Am I worthy enough to express an opinion? Compared with all the articulate and talented people in the world, will anyone care what I feel?

In a sense, efficacy is an aspect of a person's view of himself; trust is a perception of something outside of himself, the political system. Obviously the two are intertwined and, in America, a person who trusts the system is usually also a well-educated person with a high sense of personal efficacy. But to an extent, efficacy and trust are also separate. To give an example, suppose we have a country where decisions are made by leadership groups far detached from individual inputs. In a system like this, the more informed and educated a person is, the more likely that person is to know that decisions are not made by individuals but by leaders. As education rises, the feeling that the government is responsive to the individual will decline. At the same time, the person's high levels of information (and perhaps formal education) will create more confidence and assertiveness, hence raising the person's efficacy level.[31]

In Table 2.17 we report several measures of alienation. As the reader can see, levels of alienation on these items vary from a high of 73% to a low of 18%. The high level of agree responses on the first item ("Government and politics are too complicated for the average person to understand") seems to indicate an awe for the complexity of modern society. One person observed that "Even politicans don't know what is going on." Many respondents seem intimidated by politics. But this feeling is not simply a function of low educational levels or low interest, as many behavioral scientists would have us believe. While it is disproportionately concentrated in low socio-economic groups and the less informed, it is a feeling shared by many others as well. It often conceals not simply an incapacity to understand but a sense of frustration and anger that something so important is so beyond them. Some people blame politicians themselves for their dilemma, such as the man who angrily asserted "They *make* it complicated!" Others fix their anger on the media.

Slightly over half (55%) feel that news reporting is biased and unfair. From this we can surmise that much of the television audience views what they receive with skepticism. Whether this is partially a result of the Nixon-era attacks on television news is not clear.

Perhaps equally important, many of those who disagreed with the accusation of bias felt they were getting poor reporting. One man said news was, on the whole, truthful, but added: "I always make a point to look behind what is printed . . . I would say the news is distorted more than biased." One critic saw the media as taking sides in conflict among political leaders: "It is biased for the guy they want elected." Another saw the media as supporting a united power elite: "They are pro-establishment in what is written about and what is restrained." A third revealed a degree of confusion and frustration: "We are being brainwashed. I don't know who is behind it. But there is no truth." Other comments were more sympathetic of the harried world of news reporters: "They may not give all the news but they give what they think is important." And one man saw the news media as marketing a product, and blamed the people themselves for the news coverage they got: "The important news doesn't get out. People are more interested in murder."

Leaving the question of information and the news media, we turn to another major institution which links the individual to the govern-

TABLE 2.17
Measures of Alienation

Item	Alienation Level (%)
Government and politics are too complicated for the average person to understand	73
Most news reports are biased and unfair	55
Parties are run for the benefit of the few	52
Politicians can be trusted to do what they believe is right	51
Public officials don't care what people like me think	48
Politicians thermometer. Percent below 50	48
The average person can't do anything about public affairs	30
People have no say in government decisions	26
Voting is not important	18

ment—the political parties. Their importance to the functioning of the political system is hard to overestimate. They transmit public opinion upward; they mediate between bureaucracies and citizens; they link together diverse elements of the population in a common organization. If, for any reason, parties do not perform their functions in the eyes of the public, the system would break down. To measure attitudes on this topic, we asked four questions which related to parties, politicians, and officials. All four of these showed that about half of all respondents had serious reservations about the groups and individuals concerned. One item, "Both major parties in this country are controlled by small groups of men and run for their benefit," (an agree/disagree item) led with 52% alienation. The statement that "most politicians can be trusted to do what they think is best for the country" prompted 51% disagreement. Forty eight percent agree that "I don't think public officials care much about what people like me think", and an identical 48% rated politicians below 50° on the feeling thermometer.

This sense of distrust of politicians and political structures seems to be an important aspect of community values. Respondents spoke to us in angry and aggressive terms about their leaders. Part of this, of course, may be simply a natural process of grumbling and complaining.

In a big, complex society people see their representatives at a distance and feel a certain detachment from them. Quite naturally they point a finger of blame when something goes wrong—as it has done periodically over the past decade. But to understand what these attitudinal patterns mean for the political system we must delve deeper than simple grumbling. One thing which is clear is that these attitudes do not indicate a permanent withdrawal from politics. While disproportionately concentrated in the non-participants, alienation includes Democrats and Republicans, the informed and uninformed, identifiers and independents. We spoke to well-informed party identifiers who never miss an election who were still alienated. We also spoke to alienated non-voters. We should not conclude that these alienated people are permanently out of the political system. They represent a mass of latent participants waiting for some issue or personality to mobilize them. And while we do not wish to ignore the 50% or so on each item who indicate feelings of trust for the system, we feel that the alienated half of the population is the critical group. It is they who have little loyalty to the parties, little loyalty to their leaders, little loyalty to the whole process of decision making. They could move rapidly across the political system in an unpredictable direction.

On the question of voting ("Some people say voting is really not very important. Do you agree or disagree with that?"), we find a most enthusiastic response pattern, with over 82% showing pro-system feelings. Closely linked to this in both response pattern and underlying logic is the agree/disagree item, "People like me don't have any say about how the government runs things." Based on the comments which people made when asked this question, it seems that many were thinking in terms of voting as a means of expression. In other words, many people feel they have no control over government decisions and they cling to the vote as an ultimate weapon to use against politicians. Thus both alienated and non-alienated respondents endorse voting. The non-alienated see it as a means of maintaining control of the political system; the alienated as a final check upon the abuse of power.

Other respondents who felt that something was amiss with the political system focused their attention less upon politicians and more upon the citizens. To them the major problem was nonparticipation. "It's our own fault. If we got involved and paid attention these things wouldn't happen," said one respondent in reference to the Watergate affair. Another, echoing the same sentiments felt that "if everybody voted, things would be different." Another critic of the political system who seemed to enjoy his task as armchair analyst and did not want to risk his credibility by staying at home on election day concluded by observing, "you can't bitch if you don't vote."

Finally, there are those people who insist that voting is not important. Such people display a profound distrust of the political system and its ability to respond to their needs. One interesting subgroup of these—not large in number but large enough to draw our attention and warrant an observation—are those who have repudiated presidential voting because of the alleged undemocratic nature of the Electoral College. Enough people mentioned this specific institution that we feel it deserves notice. While as political scientists we are not convinced that the direct election of the president would be more democratic than the present indirect system, enough respondents volunteered this observation to make it worthy of note.

In conclusion, we find a variable pattern of alienation but one which focused sometimes on big business, sometimes on labor unions, sometimes upon the media and sometimes the parties. Highest support is for the right of voting, but even here we sense that many think of voting as a means of controlling the power of elected officials rather than of a chance to pick someone to advance their interests. Such a high level of alienation suggests that, in a large proportion of the public, the trust and attachment which binds people together is not present.

CHAPTER 3: Values in Conflict

All the attitudes examined in our study of party realignment and disintegration can be grouped into two basic clusters. The first cluster we call the Alignment Cluster because it is associated with the persistent voting patterns of the New Deal. Its components are Party Identification and New Deal social welfare liberalism. The second cluster we call the Disintegration Cluster because it encompasses attitudes which cut across party lines and hence destabilize the party system. It is made up of Law and Order, the Inglehart value system, Racial Prejudice, Racial Fears, and Life Style. The Alignment Cluster and the Disintegration Cluster are almost completely unrelated to each other. They are "nearly decomposable" in the language of cognitive psychologists.[1] Simply stated, then, the fact that a person is liberal on the Alignment Cluster does not tell us whether that person will be liberal or conservative on the Disintegration Cluster. For our purposes, a person's mind can be split into two distinct parts because the individual does not make any connection between attitudes in the Disintegration Cluster and those in the Alignment Cluster.

In this chapter we would like to do several things: we would like to show how, through the use of a statistical technique called factor analysis, we established the existence of the two main attitude clusters just mentioned; we would like to show how these two main clusters are broken into several sub-sets of attitudes; we would like to show how these sub-sets of attitudes are linked to each other; and we would like to discuss in detail several of the individual issue-items which seem to have a particular impact on public opinion. A full discussion of how these issue dimensions are linked to voting behavior appears in chapter five.

The Attitude Structure

To discover how the numerous attitudes discussed in chapter two are linked together, we turned to factor analysis, a statistical technique which classifies attitudes into "factors" or groupings of opinions which are so intercorrelated as to be measuring the same underlying concept.[2] For example, a factor analysis of the Dearborn study reveals that the thermometer items on black militants and urban rioters are associated together (hence they "load" on the same factor). This means that they are measuring some common trait. Once a factor analysis has determined what questions load on a factor, the analyst must determine what that underlying trait is. The analyst must make an educated guess, based on what the questions seem to have in common, as to what the factor represents in the minds of respondents. We have chosen to call the above factor containing black militants and urban rioters the Racial Fears factor. An individual would be high or low on the factor according to whether he reflected much fear (low opinions of black militants and urban rioters) or little fear.

Once a factor analysis has identified a group of questions that are associated together, it is then possible to use any one of the questions as an indicator of people's feelings about that concept. For example, people's responses to the thermometer item, "black militants," can be used as a general indication of their level of Racial Fears. Their responses to "urban rioters" can be used in the same way.

Table 3.1 presents the results of a factor analysis of two dozen variables in our data set.* These two dozen questions factor into seven underlying attitude dimensions (subsections of the two clusters mentioned earlier). The numbers in the table are called factor loadings, and may be thought of as the correlation, or degree of linkage, between the specific questions and the underlying concepts, or "factors," for which the questions are indicators. A perfect one to one association would be + 1.0 or − 1.0. Note that the minus association does not show there is no relationship, but rather a negative relationship. Thus, we would guess that people who have a *high* opinion of Democrats would have a *low* opinion of Republicans. The relationship is strong but negative. A non-relationship is one which approaches 0.0, meaning that the two items are not related. In the case of factor analysis the higher the loading, the better the question serves as a measure of the concept. A question is identified with the factor with which it has the highest loading.

---

*These variables were selected on the grounds that they might affect the voters' choice in the 1972 or 1976 presidential election. Some of the analysis of these attitude dimensions and how they changed across time first appeared in "The Structure and Stability of Political Attitudes: Findings From the 1974–76 Dearborn Panel Study," *Public Opinion Quarterly* 40 (1983), by the authors.

TABLE 3.1
Factor analysis of key questionnaire items

Factors:	1. Racial Prejudice	2. New Deal	3. New Morality	4. Law & Order	5. Parti- sanship	6. Post- Materialism	7. Racial Fears
Blacks	*.78*	.03	.08	-.04	.07	.03	.07
Intermarriage	*-.35*	.00	.28	.24	-.01	-.15	-.02
Black employment	*.27*	.06	-.09	-.21	.06	.07	.15
Income welfare	.07	*.72*	-.08	-.07	-.06	.05	.00
Job welfare	.08	*.55*	.12	-.03	-.14	.01	.02
Health welfare	.00	*.55*	-.02	.03	-.08	-.03	-.07
Housing welfare	-.09	*.44*	.03	.09	-.11	-.03	-.10
Marijuana users	.07	-.05	*-.69*	-.15	.02	.10	.35
Homosexuals	.17	.05	*-.43*	-.12	-.08	.13	.26
Sex education	.18	.08	*-.43*	-.11	-.09	.08	.00
X-rated films	.06	.01	*.43*	.21	-.16	-.13	-.05
Abortion	.08	.05	*.36*	.05	-.06	-.02	.01
Women's liberation	.23	-.16	*-.26*	-.10	-.02	.16	.17
Capital punishment	-.12	.15	.07	*.51*	-.01	-.12	-.02
Wallace	.00	-.13	.05	*.44*	.12	-.09	-.02
Judges too soft	.03	-.01	-.17	*-.40*	.11	.00	.13
Police search	-.07	.04	-.25	*-.33*	.18	.13	.08
Busing	-.09	.15	.08	*.31*	-.06	-.24	-.23
Gun registration	.07	-.01	-.06	*-.22*	-.04	.01	-.04
Party identification	-.06	.32	-.02	-.06	*-.76*	-.09	.00
Party thermometer difference	-.06	.22	-.10	.02	*-.69*	-.08	-.05
Inglehart #2	.08	-.01	-.14	-.11	.01	*.74*	.09
Inglehart #1	.06	-.02	-.15	-.13	.11	*.49*	.02
Urban rioters	.05	-.09	-.21	.04	.00	.00	*.75*
Black militants	.21	-.16	-.07	-.25	.12	.18	*.46*

*Varimax rotation.
Italicized numbers indicate the factor with which an item is most strongly associated.

The first factor we call Racial Prejudice because it has measures of attitudes towards blacks associated with it. A second factor called New Deal includes questions about government economic help in income, jobs, medicine, and housing. A third factor, New Morality, focuses on unconventional or non-traditional social behavior. Law and Order, the fourth factor, deals with crime and social disorder. A fifth factor, Partisanship, focuses on attitudes towards the parties. A sixth factor includes the two measures of the Inglehart value hierarchy, which we call Post-Materialism. The final factor, already discussed, is Racial Fears.

If each of these factors represents a basic underlying attitude, it is important to understand how these attitudes are correlated, or clustered together. This can be done by examining Table 3.2. This table shows that there are two clusters of factors. The first cluster is made up of attitudes on New Deal and on Partisanship. New Deal is uncorrelated with any of the five other issue dimensions. This means liberalism or conservatism on this dimension is unrelated to liberalism or conservatism on race, life style, or law and order issues. But New Deal is correlated with Partisanship, showing that the political parties are still seen by the voters in terms of the historic New Deal issues. Partisanship itself is weakly associated with Racial Fears $(-.16)$ and Post-Materialism $(-.12)$, showing that Republicans are slightly more prone to racial fear and to materialism than Democrats. But there are no partisan differences on Racial Prejudice, New Morality, or Law and Order. Partisanship and New Deal values are strongly correlated with each other as a first cluster.

The second cluster contains the other five factors, the ones identified as new issues of the 1960's and 1970's. Nine out of ten possible correlations within the Disintegration Cluster are high while only two out of ten of the possible correlations across the two clusters are even moderately high. In terms of our realignment framework, we have statistically identified a Disintegration Cluster of five interrelated, cross-cutting issues, each of which is basically at right angles to (uncorrelated with) the New Deal partisanship Alignment Cluster.

The Racial Dimension

The Alignment Cluster is a long recognized and thoroughly researched cluster of opinions. We will not dwell at length on it here. The Disintegration Cluster is a newer and less documented cluster whose existence has only recently been described.[3] We want to devote

TABLE 3.2
*Correlations between primary factors**

Racial Prejudice	Racial Prejudice	New Deal	New Morality	Law and Order	Partisan-ship	Post-Materialism
New Deal	−.02					
New Morality	.06	.00				
Law and Order	.21	.00	.33			
Parti-sanship	−.01	.20	−.04	−.09		
Post-Materialism	.21	−.05	.23	.30	−.12	
Racial Fears	.19	−.08	.19	.20	−.16	.21

*This table was obtained through an OBLIMIN rotation in OSIRIS III using a gamma coefficient of 0.5.

some attention to the Disintegration Cluster to bring out some new information on it.

We begin with an issue that many people would like to ignore but which is central to the politics of the 1970s—black-white relations. The question of race has divided the American public more than any other issue in the past and has contributed significantly to the disruption of American party systems. The realignment of the 1850's was primarily based on the question of the legal status of the black man in America. The realignment of the 1890's failed to produce a united populist democratic front in part because of the split within the populists over black-white relations. In the 1930's, Roosevelt succeeded in wooing away many black votes from their Republican moorings with his social and welfare policies.

In the 1960's and 1970's, race-related issues likewise dominated events. In the early 1960's the civil rights movement, concentrated in the South, grabbed most of the headlines; by the early 1960's urban riots—northern, and mostly occurring in black inner cities—became paramount; following this were issues of crime and drugs, not racial, to be sure, but seen by many whites as race-related. Finally, in the 1970's was the matter of school busing to achieve racial balance, an issue which more clearly dealt with black-white interaction than any issue since the earlier civil rights movement. The main difference between the busing

TABLE 3.3
Factor analysis of racial questions.*

| | Factors | | |
| | I | II | III |
Questions	Prejudice	Racial Fears	White Response
Blacks	.53	.11	.08
Black employment	.49	.10	−.18
Intermarriage	−.48	−.08	.18
Advice to blacks	−.27	−.07	.08
Race major issue	−.20	−.02	−.05
Black militants	.17	.75	−.12
Urban rioters	.10	.45	.00
Wallace	−.03	.03	.47
Busing	−.06	−.28	.42

*Varimax rotation.
Italicized items load on the factor indicated.

issue of the 1970's and the school desegregation efforts of the 1950's and 1960's was that the earlier efforts were designed to break up *Southern, de jure* segregation, which often took children outside of their neighborhood to attend segregated schools. Desegregation in that context tended to uphold the neighborhood school concept, although in some cases where *de jure* residential segregation was found, busing out of neighborhoods was used. In the late 1960's and early 1970's, however, school desegregation focused on *Northern, de facto* segregation which was based upon custom or coercion but not necessarily law. The issue thus polarized and threatened to split the northern Democratic coalition. To gain a fresh perspective on exactly how this polarization occurred and what it meant, we conducted a factor analysis of the nine racial items discussed in chapter two. What emerged from that analysis was a three dimensional solution (see Table 3.3). This means that there is not simply one set of racial attitudes, but three sets, which, while related to an extent, are largely distinct from each other. The first of these dimensions is an expanded version of what we have already called Racial Prejudice. It consists of the thermometer item on blacks, the question on the causes of black unemployment, opinion of interracial marriage, and the advice one would give blacks who want to get ahead. A cold feeling toward blacks, a tendency to blame black unemployment on inherent black deficiencies, opposition to intermarriage, and negative advice to blacks who want to get ahead all went together in a broad pattern of prejudice.

A second dimension of racial attitudes revolved around Racial Fear.

71

Figure 3.1 Racial Prejudice and Racial Fears (Varimax Rotation)

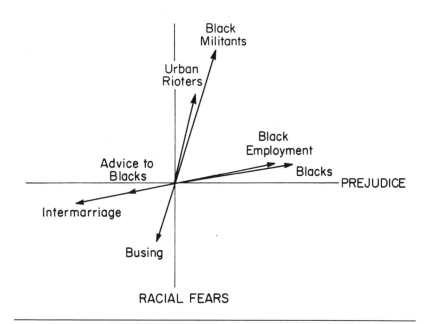

Black militants and urban rioters were strongly associated with this dimension, and concern about busing was also associated with it. Busing had not loaded on the earlier prejudice dimension, and there was little connection between opposition to busing and negative feelings towards blacks. Opinions on busing seem more associated with fear of violence than with prejudice *per se,* as can be seen in Figure 3.1.

These two dimensions tend to be associated, as can be seen graphically by the fact that they incline towards each other rather than being at right angles. But even though people who score high on Racial Fear tend to score high on Racial Prejudice, the two dimensions are distinct. Many people who are unprejudiced are high on racial fear; others who are prejudiced are low on racial fear.

The third dimension of racial attitudes involves the white response to blacks. Attitudes associated with this pattern are support for George Wallace and opposition to busing. The reader will recall from the comprehensive factor analysis with which we began this chapter that these two attitudes are associated with capital punishment, judges too soft, and police search, in a dimension we called law and order. That

72

dimension correlated equally (r = .2) with Racial Prejudice and Racial Fears, showing that law and order attitudes have a basis both in racial prejudice and in racial fears.

This overlap between law and order and racial dimensions raises the question as to exactly how different or similar the two sets of attitudes are. Is fear of crime in the white community merely an overflow of anti-black feeling? Are people able to distinguish in their minds between criminals, blacks, and black criminals? To answer these questions we again turned to the computer, asking it to combine racial items with crime and social disorder items, and to search for patterns.

The patterns which emerged (Table 3.4) show that law and order/ social disruption attitudes are powerful and independent, but are affected by considerations of race. In addition to the re-emergence of the racial fears and law and order dimensions we see a new attitude pattern which we call "vigilante." This dimension has on it support for Archie Bunker and George Wallace and opposition to handgun registration. It has no directly racial item. A second new dimension we call "conventionalism." We are admittedly confused about the true meaning of this factor because it is made up of people who are strongly supportive of both police and blacks, items which could conceivably be inconsistent.

The thrust of this table however is quite clear: we are not dealing with a simple single dimension but with a complex mixture of racial prejudice, fear, and law and order. The breadth of the issues involved makes them in toto very critical in the political system. Their complexity, however, makes them tend to be amorphous and hard to focus. A simple reduction to racism, for example, would split away those people who are not anti-black in their sentiments. To these researchers the single item which linked together prejudice, fear, and law and order was the problem of busing. We believe that busing, as much as any other issue, summarized the frustrations, fears, prejudices, and angers of the modern periurban man. To understand our contemporary political system, at either a local or at a national level, we must look in detail at busing.

This, however, is not a simple task. Earlier researchers had reported mostly "negative findings" in the busing area: it was easy to know what did not cause busing attitudes, but it was harder to say what did cause them.[4] Kelley found that racism correlated very highly with age, education and income (as previous research would lead us to suspect), but he found significantly weaker relations between busing attitudes and the same characteristics. If busing and racism are closely related

TABLE 3.4
*Variables associated with law and order and racial factors**

	Factors			
Variables	Racial Fears	Convention- alism	Law & Order	Vigilante
Black militants	.65	.10	.28	−.12
Urban rioters	.59	−.05	.05	.05
Police	−.26	.77	−.16	.13
Blacks	.21	.41	.05	−.19
Capital punishment	−.04	−.02	−.55	.19
Judges soft	.13	.02	.44	−.05
Busing	−.25	.09	−.36	.08
Police search	.14	−.22	.33	−.11
Archie Bunker	−.14	−.03	−.03	.68
Wallace	.01	.20	−.33	.38
Gun control	−.05	.03	.14	−.26

*Varimax rotation.
Italicized items load on the factor indicated.

issues (as Kelley had expected) they should show similar patterns when compared with the same variables. Kelley also found a surprisingly weak relationship between integration attitudes and busing attitudes, a result which suggests that busing is a part of some nearly non-racial attitude dimension.

In examining busing in Dearborn we take into account three possible reasons for opposing it.

1. Racial attitudes. Most commonly, opponents of busing are described as "racists" or "bigots." Quite logically, a white who disliked blacks would also dislike busing because of the integration overtones of the policy. The research of Kelley and the fact that anti-busing attitudes are so universally held leads us to doubt that this would provide a complete explanation. If racial attitudes do link closely with busing, then busing should be part and parcel with other aspects of the racial dimensions, and with other attitudes and characteristics known to co-vary with them, such as ethnocentrism, low education, low income, and intolerance of diversity.

2. Law and order attitudes. To many residents of the suburbs, the urban areas are places to be feared and avoided. When asked to comment on the major problem facing the metropolitan area, most of our respondents mentioned crime, drugs, racial tensions, and other similar issues. When asked about busing, many of those giving reasons for

their opposition listed the same sorts of matters. It is entirely possible that the bulk of anti-busing feeling is not a result of anti-black sentiment but simply fear of moving one's children out of a safe neighborhood school into what is perceived as a less safe one. Certainly, in many cases this fear would be unwarranted. Urban schools are not necessarily less safe than suburban ones, and should not be stereotyped. But fears are not always rational and it seems very likely that racial fears are a major aspect of anti-busing sentiment.

3. Finally, there is the possibility that the busing controversy is not a simple matter of race or law and order, but that it is a much more complex matter. This is a time of great cultural ferment. Social disruption is massive. Families are breaking up. Fundamental religious and social values are being rejected. During such a time it is only logical that people would seek to hold what they have. A time of social change is one which usually generates revival or restoration movements, movements usually called "reactionary" by their detractors. These movements seek to preserve and salvage the old culture, often by a focus upon the young or the females of society (who are seen as the base of the future value system), by an effort to preserve the family structure or save traditional social units, or by a focus upon some symbolic issue which sums up or represents the conflict between traditional and anti-traditional value systems. Later in the chapter we will show that this approach is a very useful one for understanding the busing (but not necessarily the racial) issue.

The volatility of the busing issue could be measured by the exploding fire bombs and burning buses of nearby Pontiac. At the same time the first wave of this study was conducted in 1974, Dearborn and the whole of the Detroit area was under a court-ordered busing plan to be implemented the following fall. Politicians in the suburbs, many of them old-time liberals, were scrambling to get onto the anti-busing bandwagon. Wallace had carried the area in the 1972 Democratic primary on a strong anti-busing platform. There was no doubt in our minds that our respondents would be strongly anti-busing, and, as seen in chapter two, our expectations were correct. Only 6% of our respondents even mildly favored busing, and 65% were strongly opposed. Clearly busing was a powerful issue. Our purpose, however, was not merely to establish that fact (since it was already known), but to go a step further and find out why the particular issue was so emotional when others (such as open housing laws) often were introduced with minimal disruption.

75

TABLE 3.5
Attitudes on busing by black thermometer scores

Busing	Black Thermometer Scores		
	51–100	50	0–49
Favor and strongly favor	9%	6%	3%
Oppose	27%	29%	25%
Strongly oppose	64%	64%	71%
	N = 229	N = 140	N = 63

Kendall's Tau B = .05 Significance = .08

The Busing Issue

We began our analysis by comparing busing attitudes with attitudes toward blacks. As seen in Table 3.5, there is no significant relationship. Ninety-seven percent of those with negative feelings about blacks oppose busing, while 93% of those with positive feelings oppose busing. The correlation coefficient establishes what the percentages indicate: the relationship between the two attitudes is not a strong one.

If there is no relationship between attitudes towards blacks and attitudes towards busing, does busing relate to other racial attitudes? Tables 3.6 and 3.7 show the relationship between busing and the items on black unemployment and interracial marriage. The first of these shows a link between placing blame for black unemployment on blacks and opposition to busing. The correlation is + .14. The item on intermarriage is more strongly related to busing. The correlation there is + .18. Interestingly, the major differences are not between those for and against busing but rather between those strongly opposed to it, and the others. Respondents who disapprove of intermarriage or who feel it is morally wrong are noticeably more likely to be strong opponents of busing, while others are more likely to merely oppose it. It seems clear that persons who oppose intermarriage are especially afraid of busing, perhaps not so much out of fear that blacks and whites will not get along, but out of fear that they will get along too well.

Overall, the average correlation between racial items and busing in our study is .12, exactly the same magnitude as found by Kelley in his earlier work. These findings seem to suggest that attitudes on busing are linked with overall racial attitudes, but only loosely so.

Further evidence of this is seen when we look at the social location of busing attitudes. Most studies of racism, intolerance, and other related

TABLE 3.6
Attitudes on busing by attitudes on the causes of black unemployment

	Causes of Black Unemployment	
Busing	System Blame	Personal Blame
Favor and strongly favor	9%	4%
Oppose	31%	22%
Strongly oppose	58%	42%
	N = 268	N = 161

Kendall's Tau B = .14 Significance = .00

TABLE 3.7
Attitudes on busing by attitudes on interracial marriage

	Attitudes on Interracial Marriage			
Busing	Personal Matter	Think Carefully	Disapprove	Morally Wrong
Favor and strongly favor	16%	7%	4%	4%
Oppose	28%	33%	24%	15%
Strongly oppose	56%	61%	72%	81%
	N = 99	N = 162	N = 100	N = 74

Kendall's Tau B = .18 Significance = .00

attitudes find that such dimensions are an inverse function of socio-economic status (SES) levels. Persons with lower education, lower income, or lower status jobs are more likely to be intolerant or prejudiced. Likewise, persons who are older are more characterized by such attitudes than persons who are younger.[5] Table 3.8 shows a similar relationship. Opposition to interracial marriage and personal blame responses on the unemployment question are characteristic of older persons in lower SES levels. All six correlations are statistically significant.

Busing attitudes on the other hand, are not so clearly related to these background characteristics. Correlations of busing with age and with income are not statistically significant, though opposition to busing is associated with lower education. These findings are very similar to those reported earlier in which Kelley concluded that low SES was associated with prejudice, but that the relation of SES to busing was much less obvious.

It is clear then that a fuller understanding of the busing issue must lie in the wider political realm. As seen in chapter two, our questionnaire

TABLE 3.8
Some correlations with busing and with prejudice

	Busing	Racial Intermarriage	Causes of Black Unemployment
Black militants	−.27	−.20	−.16
Marijuana smokers	−.26	−.24	−.18
Capital punishment	.24	.21	.10
Ronald Reagan	.23	.13	.02*
X-rated films	−.21	−.15	−.10
Materialist Values (second set)	−.21	−.21	−.12
Homosexuals	−.20	−.15	−.02*
Policemen	.20		
Whites	.19	.12	.08
Interracial marriage	.18	1.00	.27
George Wallace	.18	.08	.12
The military	.18	.15	.16
Urban rioters	−.18	−.07*	−.15
Women's liberation movement	−.17	−.11	−.12
Archie Bunker	.06*	.34	.24
Black unemployment	.12	.27	1.00
Blacks	.06*	.23	−.30
Sex education	−.08*	−.23	−.09
Children who talk back	−.15	−.21	−.16
Busing	1.00	.21	.12
Voting is the only way	−.08	−.19	−.18
Liberals	−.14	−.18	−.18
Police search	−.12	−.17	−.18
Peaceful protest OK	.11	.15	.19
Taxes to reduce pollution	.10	.12	.19
Limits on free speech	−.08*	−.14	−.17
Age	.03*	.18	−.13
Education	−.10	−.13	.10
Income	−.01*	−.06	.14

*Relations not significant at the .05 level. Correlations are Pearson's R.

covered a broad spectrum of political topics. We assessed attitudes on 10 major national political figures, 20 groups of people (such as whites, Jews, Catholics, big business and politicians), New Deal programs, civil liberties, political efficacy and trust, law and order, race relations, and changing mores. Table 3.8 presents those items that correlated most highly with busing.

Opposition to busing was most strongly associated with negative feelings toward culturally deviant, anti-traditional, non-conventional groups and practices: black militants and marijuana smokers, X-rated films, homosexuals, interracial marriage, urban rioters, and women's liberation. Symbols of militant defense of convention are equally associated with opposition to busing: support of capital punishment and positive feelings toward Ronald Reagan and George Wallace, the police, and the military. Rounding out the list are positive attitudes toward whites and adherence to a materialist value system. The portrait of the busing opponent that emerges is not one of racism but one of militant, entrenched defense of community values in the face of an onslaught of black militants, marijuana smokers, smut purveyors (X-rated movies), homosexuals, and destroyers of conventional family life (interracial marriage and women's liberation).

Items correlating highly with racial prejudice are different from those correlating highly with busing. For example, items correlating most highly with the black unemployment question are the thermometer on blacks and opinion on interracial marriage. These, we have argued above, are measures of prejudice. Interestingly, their correlations with busing are relatively low.

Thus, while there is some relationship between racial attitudes and busing, we do not feel that one can adequately understand the busing controversy by looking at it merely as a racial matter. While race plays a role in the anti-busing movement, skin color is a relatively insignificant component of the overall conflict. There is a much broader matter of fundamental value systems at the heart of the issue. To the extent that blacks do not fit into this value system, race may be important. More important, however, is the fact that in a time of confusion and social ferment, the movement of children physically out of their neighborhood makes it increasingly difficult for parents to control not only their children but the institutions of socialization which are shaping the future. During the study of Dearborn, there were in quick succession two major regional social upheavals: a textbook boycott in Kanawa County, West Virginia, and anti-busing riots in Boston. While one of these occurred in small-town, Protestant, hill country in the south and the other occurred in the Catholic, urban north, we feel that both are manifestations of the same phenomenon. The onslaught of a counter-culture has challenged the basic beliefs and institutions of society. Increasingly people's destiny is being taken over by distant bureaucrats, experts, technicians, the media, intellectuals, and other groups and forces over which individuals have no control. Logically, they are making their stand in the schools where the future is being shaped. The yellow school bus, which for generations of Americans symbolized the best in the traditional value system, came to symbolize the unwelcome intrusion of a distant, alien, and very frightening set of forces. The direction of social change and who will control it is a more critical determinant of busing attitudes than racial prejudice.

79

The New Morality

This issue of social change brings us from race and law and order to another dimension of the Disintegration Cluster—the New Morality: marijuana, homosexuals, women's liberation, X-rated films, sex education and abortion. The two most crystalized attitudes of all New Morality items are those involving marijuana use and abortion. Marijuana use, as can be seen from its dramatic link with other items in Table 3.9, is a core item. What it and other New Morality items seem to have in common (apart from sexual overtones) is an emphasis on liberation from, or breaking down of, social controls and/or inhibitions. For example, marijuana use is often advocated as a means of psychological relaxation and of liberating the mind. Its proponents cite it as a means of "forgetting" or of temporarily "dropping out." As such, it is a symbol of social defiance and the rejection of conventional norms. Abortion attitudes, on the other hand, are the least related to the others because abortion injects a right-to-life issue into the debate, and thus becomes the only one of the New Morality issues under consideration that contains a potential victim. This confounding factor perhaps explains why the lowest correlation in the table is between abortion and women's liberation, two issues which might have been seen as a natural pair.

As shown in chapter five, women's liberation is the best predictor of presidential voting of all the New Morality items. But the Women's Liberation Movement symbolizes much more than feminist aspiration to Dearbornites, and this may account for its cool reception (49° thermometer). Items linked closely to women's liberation (see Table 3.10) include the politicians' thermometer, the liberals' thermometer, self-actualization, and the black militants and urban rioters thermometers. It is also not surprising, in the aftermath of the McGovern Democratic convention, with its quota system and its demonstrating minorities, that McGovern's thermometer was highly correlated with the women's liberation thermometer. It would seem that, to many people, women's liberation is closely associated with negatively viewed protesters, like black militants or urban rioters, or neutrally valued politicians and liberals. This is not intended as a criticism of feminist leadership since dramatic tactics are often required to get a response from the political system.[6] But the dramatic politicization of this issue transformed it into a symbol powerful enough to affect the presidential election, by accentuating the disintegration of the Democratic coalition.

TABLE 3.9
*Correlations within the New Morality Factor**

	Women's Liberation	Homosexuals	Abortion	Marijuana Users	Sex Education	X-Rated
Women's Liberation	1.0					
Homosexuals	.18	1.0				
Abortion	-.12	-.15	1.0			
Marijuana Users	.32	.45	-.23	1.0		
Sex Education	.20	.25	-.16	.30	1.0	
X-Rated	-.16	-.16	.14	-.38	-.22	1.0

*Correlations are Pearson's R. All are significant at .001.

TABLE 3.10
*Some correlations with the
women's liberation
thermometer**

Marijuana users	.32
McGovern	.31
Politicians	.30
Liberals	.26
Self-actualization	.23
Black militants	.23
Blacks	.22
Sex education	.21
Homosexuals	.20
Urban rioters	.19
Judges too soft	.19
Ted Kennedy	.19
Young people	.17
Busing	−.17
X-Rated	−.14
Abortion	.11

*Correlations are Pearson's R.
All are significant at .01 level.

Materialist Value Hierarchy

The final element of the Disintegration Cluster is the Inglehart value hierarchy. This is the simplest of the factors to describe, since the two items loading on it are both measures of post-materialism analyzed by Inglehart,[7] and others,[8] and discussed in detail in chapter two. Inglehart asserts that these items are designed to measure a person's basic values. Rokeach, in a classic work, suggests that values should be (1) relatively durable basic beliefs (2) from which many specific attitudes are derived or inferred.[9] Taking these two characteristics of values into account, do we have reason to think that Inglehart has succeeded in measuring basic underlying values, or is he measuring just another attitude? This is important to us as we attempt to understand the Disintegration Cluster. We have already seen (Table 3.2) that the Inglehart factor is correlated about equally (r=.2) with all four of the other factors in the Disintegration Cluster. Should it then be interpreted as in some sense "causing" the other factors? This would make sense if it measures an underlying value from which attitudes on Racial, New Morality, and Law and Order factors could in some sense be inferred. On the other hand, all five factors in the Disintegration Cluster might be a coequal and mutually supporting system of attitudes. This would make sense if the Inglehart factor were simply measuring another attitude. We do not have the data to definitively answer this question but we can approach an answer by returning to the characteristics of values we have just mentioned. In relation to the first characteristic (stability over time), Inglehart reports that the first panel data on the subject showed that his measures of values are not very stable.[10] Thirty-nine percent of the respondents changed their value type in a twelve month period. Inglehart argues that this is due to measurement error that results when people are asked for the first or second time in their lives to describe their basic values in a closed-ended question. He also points out that the correlation in his index was higher from one year's response to the next than is the case of most of the attitudes in the survey. We will examine this issue in our discussion of change in the next chapter and conclude that the Inglehart items do in fact measure values.

In relation to the second characteristic of values, that they should be the basis from which many attitudes are derived, we have some evidence that the Inglehart items do measure underlying values: they are moderately correlated with a truly impressive variety of attitudes. One might say that it is a rare attitude in our survey that is not significantly correlated with them.

As one can see in Table 3.11, the hierarchy, like busing and women's liberation, is strongly associated with new forces/old values items discussed earlier. A novel case in point is that the highest correlation is with preferences in the mayoral race in neighboring Detroit. This race was between a radical black, destined to become the first non-white mayor of the city, and a former police chief. What more symbolic contest could we have than a contest between the perceived enemy of traditional values and their savior-hero-protagonist?[11] Also highly correlated are such items as the thermometers on black militants, marijuana users, women's liberation and homosexuals, the thermometers on Nixon and Reagan, and an item on children talking back to their parents designed to elicit evidence of "authoritarianism".[12]

The Disintegration Cluster and Party Identification

Where did the social ferment leave the political parties? As we saw at the opening of this chapter, the parties were somewhat isolated from the culture change by the tendency of the citizens to compartmentalize their thinking. Voters had two clusters of attitudes: first, attitudes towards the New Deal and the party system; second, attitudes towards law and order, the new morality, and race relations. This dual clustering impeded the likelihood of a realignment, while at the same time

TABLE 3.11
*Some correlations with Inglehart indicators**

	Post-Bourgeois (First set)	Self-Actualization (Second set)
Detroit mayoral race	.21	.27
Black militants	.16	.24
Marijuana	.18	.22
Women's liberation	.16	.23
Reagan	−.18	−.21
Nixon	−.17	−.20
Homosexuals	.18	.18
Authoritarianism low (children talk back)	.17	.18
Police search	.13	.21
Busing	−.12	−.21
Police	−.16	−.16
The military	−.12	−.20
Liberals	.15	.15
Sex education	.12	.15
Free speech	.16	.08
Teacher hair	.09	.14

*All significant at the .05 level. Correlations are Pearson's R.

increasing the likelihood of party system disintegration by making parties irrelevant to many of the voters' new concerns. Republican party leaders, however, remained hopeful of a realignment, and thought they might provoke one by continual politicization of the new issues and exploitation of divisions within the Democratic party ranks. In this way, the existence of cross-cutting cleavages, which is often believed to be a conflict moderator, provided an opportunity for leadership groups to fan the flames of conflict to create a winning coalition.

Persistence of New Deal Issues

To Richard Nixon, the Democratic party was fragmented by ideological divisions which would soon rip it asunder. In his view, Democratic support groups such as factory workers, ethnic voters, and Catholics were no longer economically deprived and in need of government help and programs; their prosperity and middle class life style would create in them a conservative ideology and they would then be weaned away from their old commitment to federal activism. As Table 3.12 shows, this Nixon dream was simply not the case. The average percentage difference between Democrats and Republicans in terms of support for federal activism on the eight issues listed is 28%. On only two issues—encouraging low cost medical care and providing

TABLE 3.12
Party identification and support for new deal activism

% difference Democrats minus Republicans	Party Identification and . . .		Democrats	Independents	Republicans	X² significance
38	Federal housing		67	58	29	.0000
33	Government jobs		74	63	41	.0000
40	Federal medical program (1–7 scale)	+	64	44	24	.0000
		0	10	23	16	
		–	26	33	60	
28	Government income guarantee		61	47	33	.0000
24	Government quit programs		56	66	80	.0000
18	Government promote inexpensive medical care		86	92	68	.0000
29	Government jobs (1–7 scale)	+	39	13	10	.0000
		0	18	18	13	
		–	43	69	74	
15	Government aid to poor students		72	78	57	.003

educational support for poor students—do a majority of Republicans take an activist position. On every single issue but one—government jobs—Democrats provide majority support for an activist position, and even on that one issue the ratio of activists to anti-activists is over two to one. These data demonstrate the persistent potency of the linkage between partisanship and position on New Deal issues.

The place of independents in Table 3.12 is interesting to keep in mind, for non-identifiers frequently make the difference in a close election. In this table we see that non-identifiers are somewhere between Democrats and Republicans on six of the eight issues. On five of these eight issues they are closer to the Democrats in terms of percent activist. On only one of the issues are they closer to the Republicans in level of activism. On two issues—government educational loans and inexpensive medical care—they are marginally more liberal than the Democrats. Clearly, in terms of their ideology on government activism, independents average out as neither Democrat nor Republican, but somewhere in between.

The Social Issue

In the case of non-economic issues, the party pattern changes.

As discussed in detail earlier, those who saw a possibility of party realignment in the 1970's looked primarily to the newly-emergent "social issue" to provide the basis of the new cleavage. Issues of race, crime, and life style provided a set of problems on which the parties had not taken a clear position. Divisions within the parties tended to be as great as divisions across the parties. In 1968 and especially in 1972, Richard Nixon took the conservative position on these issues and induced the defection of many Democrats who were conservative on this dimension. The question remained, however, of how permanent this fracture was. With a proven conservative majority on most of these issues, it would be fatal for the Democratic coalition if the fissure occurred along party lines; if the Democratic leadership took a liberal position, then one would anticipate a permanent movement of conservative Democrats into the Republican party, thus precipitating a party realignment. If, on the other hand, the parties were divided within themselves on the issues and succeeded in blurring their position, then the result would be the defeat of individual candidates who are caught on the wrong side of the public opinion fence, but it would not precipitate a total realignment. In such a case, if the conservative majority held, we would expect both parties to move to the right on these issues, thus neutralizing their realignment *and* disintegration impact.

Tables 3.13, 3.14, and 3.15 illustrate how race, law and order, and new morality issues fit into the party system in the spring of 1976 at the time of the primaries. On two of the issue clusters (crime and race), there is a clear if not entirely unanimous conservative majority. On the life styles issues there appears to be a liberal majority. These trends were discussed earlier in chapter two and need not be repeated here. What does deserve discussion here is the way in which these issues fit within the party system. On not one single issue do we see a statistically significant difference between Democrats and Republicans (the neighborhood integration table is statistically significant, but the unreported correlation is very weak, and the significance appears to be for reasons other than party differences). Looking at the three tables together, we see that, of the total of 14 items, the Democrats are more liberal on eight of them, the Republicans more liberal on six. Thus, while George McGovern and Richard Nixon may have had different positions or images on these dimensions in 1972, the rank and file of the parties did not follow their leads.

This in itself is an interesting fact. Quite often a party leader (especially a presidential candidate) is able to lead the party faithful in the direction he would have them go. His status, his prestige, their loyalty to the party, the enthusiasm of the moment, all produce changes in how people perceive certain issues. In 1971, for example, the announcement by President Nixon that he was going to China caused Republican rank and file to make a complete turnaround on that issue, from majority opposition to increased ties with China, to majority support. The fact that this did not occur in 1972 on the issues under analysis indicates that these issues were very "hard" ones, on which people had firm, unmovable opinions. Relations with China are a matter of great complexity, on which people are willing to defer to national or party leaders; crime in the streets and racial conflict are not the same. On these issues, the rank and file view high office as evidence of detachment or lack of understanding. They themselves—the voters—are in the front lines on these issues. Where China or national security is concerned, perhaps a Ph.D. or a Georgetown address give one a certain understanding or insight into such matters; but where local security is concerned, these same qualities serve to disqualify rather than qualify their holders.

Thus, the impact of these issues—given the fact that it was candidates rather than party followers who seemed to be different on them—was to promote massive defections. The permanence of these defections would be dependent upon two factors mentioned already:

TABLE 3.13
Attitude on life style issues by party identification

	Party Difference*	Demo-crats	Indepen-dents	Repub-licans	χ^2 Signi-ficance	More Conservative Party
Pro X-rated	6	35	29	29	.44	Republicans
Woman in home	11	52	47	41	.11	Democrats
Woman president	9	70	66	61	.33	Republicans
Pro abortion	4	72	72	76	.78	Republicans
Pro sex education	15	71	88	86	.48	Democrats

*Note that none of the differences between the parties is statistically significant.

TABLE 3.14
Attitude on crime issues by party identification

	Party Difference*	Demo-crats	Indepen-dents	Repub-licans	χ^2 Signi-ficance	More Conservative Party
Pro capital punishment	9	77	90	86	.50	Democrats
Ban handguns	6	27	36	21	.15	Republicans
Pro police search	3	59	56	62	.75	Republicans
Register guns	1	88	74	79	.82	Democrats

*Note that none of the differences between the parties is statistically significant.

TABLE 3.15
Attitudes on racial issues by party identification

	Party Difference*	Demo-crats	Indepen-dents	Repub-licans	χ^2 Signi-ficance	More Conservative Party
Black unemployment (social blame)	4	64	69	68	.52	Democrats
Busing (--)	4	65	66	69	.73	Republicans
Pro intermarriage	1	57	74	58	.06	Democrats
Busing (1–4)	8	12	13	4	.25	Republicans
Neighborhood (1–4)	3	39	36	36	.04	Republicans

*Note that none of the differences between the parties is statistically significant.

Salience, or the extent to which a given issue was seen as *the* most important issue, thus driving other issues (perhaps divisive ones) out of the voters mind, and party and candidate image or the extent to which the party and its leaders (especially the nominee) are seen as being close to or far from a given voter. The image may or may not be a fair one but in the end it is the ultimate reality for the voter. If a candidate is seen as liberal, it matters not that he is a true conservative; if he is seen as an administrative incompetent, his actual brilliance in this field is irrelevant. Image assumes an existence of its own, and it is to this matter that we must now turn.

In studying a possible realignment in 1972, we were curious whether the image of the Democratic party was associated with the deviant groups so prominent in the McGovern campaign and convention. Would voters associate negatively valued reference groups such as marijuana smokers, homosexuals, women's liberation activists, and black militants with the Democratic party? If so, would middle American voters then begin to shift their votes and party allegiances to a party with whose members they felt more in common? Media coverage of the 1972 Democratic campaign and the Democratic convention had been so dominated by deviant groups of demonstrators it was possible voters would associate the Democratic party itself with the protest groups. Defining a "deviant group" as a group that received a cool thermometer rating, we asked our respondents whether members of various deviant groups were Democrats or Republicans: "The Democratic and Republican parties in this country sometimes try to attract whole groups of people to support them. Let me read you some types of people. As you see it, do you think these people are *more likely* to be in the Democratic party or the Republican party?" As can be seen in Table 3.16, where the most Democratic groups are placed at the top and the most Republican placed at the bottom, the deviant groups do tend to be somewhat associated with the Democratic party. These include black militants, marijuana users, women's lib advocates, urban rioters and homosexuals. It is perhaps noteworthy that over a third of the sample think urban rioters are Democrats. This gives the Democratic party an image problem. What saves the Democrats is that other groups with a more positive image—including policemen and young people—the two most highly regarded groups—are also identified with the Democratic party. The groups most strongly associated with the Democratic party—labor union members, blacks, liberals, Catholics, and young people—all receive a warm treatment in the thermometer ratings. So while it is true that the majority party had become

TABLE 3.16
*Popular beliefs about party identity of groups (1974)**

Group, With Thermometer Rating	Group Associated With Which Party (Percentage):				
	Demo-crats	Repub-licans	Neither, Both Equally	Don't Know	Party Difference
Labor union members, 61	77	8	2	13	69
Blacks, 60	70	8	4	19	62
Liberals, 54	62	10	5	23	52
Catholics, 68	58	7	11	24	51
Young people, 79	59	9	9	23	50
Black militants, 21	51	7	8	34	44
Marijuana users, 25	37	5	10	48	32
Women's lib advocates, 49	43	13	8	36	30
Urban rioters, 13	37	8	13	43	29
Policemen, 80	43	17	10	29	26
Homosexuals, 31	22	5	10	63	17
School teachers, 72	37	27	11	25	10
Members of the military, 66	31	27	13	29	4
Whites, 76	27	27	20	27	0
Protestants, 72	20	32	14	34	−12
Jews, 65	23	39	8	30	−16
Conservatives, 58	18	54	6	23	−36
Big business, 61	5	79	3	13	−74

*Underlined groups are those with predominantly negative ratings.

associated with deviant groups, it is also true that the party is seen as an enormous coalition embracing most of the groups mentioned in the survey. In fact, only big businessmen, conservatives, Jews, and Protestants are seen as more likely to be Republicans than Democrat; all other groups are seen as more likely to be Democrats, so a Democratic voter is not likely to feel he is in a narrow party made up of only deviants and himself. Under these circumstances, our hypothetical party identifier is more likely to take a walk for a breath of fresh air than to leave the party permanently. He is more likely to be a ticket switcher than to change party identification.

CHAPTER 4: The More Things Change, the More They Remain the Same

In this chapter we examine changes that occurred in respondent opinion in the three years of our study. We are interested in which opinions are changing and which are fixed so as to make an assessment of overall attitude and value stability. This will allow us to make some guesses about the durability of the political patterns we have been examining. In fact, we find that most opinions are not changing—marijuana, women's liberation, and trust in government are among the exceptions. In general, the attitudes and behavior we have focused upon are stable and can be expected to play an ongoing role in future elections.

Furthermore, because these attitude structures are stable, we cannot explain the vastly different 1972 and 1976 elections in terms of a public opinion shift. Most likely the different outcomes are the result of the rise and fall of certain issue clusters, some of which favor the Democrats and some of which favor the Republicans.

These shifting opinions were in part shaped by the historic events which occurred in America from 1973 to 1976. In November 1972, 15 months before the start of our study, Richard Nixon won four more years in the presidency by defeating George McGovern. Nixon was inaugurated amid great pomp in January 1973, but by the summer of 1973 the Senate Select Watergate Committee, under the Chairmanship of Sen. Sam Ervin, was investigating criminal charges against the Nixon administration. John Dean's testimony implicated the President himself in this wrongdoing. In September, 1973, further scandal rocked the Nixon administration as Vice President Spiro Agnew pled no contest to criminal charges and resigned from office. Gerald Ford became Vice President in October, 1973. Also in October, 1973, a war in the Middle East broke out, and was followed by an Arab oil embargo and a hike in oil prices—a quadrupling—by the Organization of Petroleum Exporting Countries (OPEC).

Our first wave of interviewing took place in February 1974. Shortly thereafter, the lagged effect of the embargo and price hike struck the national economy. Inflation quickened and a recession began as well. For the first time in memory, and to the bafflement of economists who advised the president, the nation's economy reeled under simultaneous recession and inflation. Seventeen and one half percent of our respondents were laid off at some time between the first and second interview (though sometimes for short periods). Soon thereafter, Richard Nixon resigned from office after being indicted by the House Judiciary Committee for impeachable offenses. Gerald Ford became president in July, 1974, and promptly pardoned Nixon.

Our second wave of interviewing occurred in February–March, 1975, after the worst of the government scandals, but in the very bottom of the economic woes. The rest of 1975 and early 1976 was a period of very gradual, unspectacular economic recovery. It was a time of behind-the-scenes political maneuvering by presidential hopefuls building campaign war chests. It was also the period of the first primary campaign—the New Hampshire presidential preference primary.

The third wave of the interviewing began the day after the New Hampshire primary and continued for about three to four weeks. Then came the successful primary campaigns of Jimmy Carter and Gerald Ford. After the 1976 presidential election, the fourth and final wave of interviewing was carried out.

Attitude Changes

To study which attitudes shifted and which did not, we used a panel study approach: we interviewed the same people from year to year, asked several questions in identical form in each year of the study, and compared the answers of individuals in one year with the answers of the same individuals in other years. We were anticipating two possible patterns of change—true change and false change. True change is that change which results from "real" shifts in public opinion. In most years, we would expect little real change, since political values tend to be fairly stable (though attitudes on specific political objects—What do you think of the president's performance this week?—are more fluid). We did, of course, find several items on which real change is occurring and these will be discussed later in the chapter.

What is more difficult, however, is locating non-real change, in particular what is sometimes called "noise." Noise refers not to problems of "validity" (does the question measure what we think it measures?) but rather to problems of "reliability" (if we ask the same person the same question twice, will we get the same answer both times, assuming the respondent has not changed positions?). The difficulty is that many people simply do not have opinions on certain issues. Such a person, being interviewed, is put in the position of admitting ignorance or of answering in spite of ignorance. Most of us will choose to answer rather than admit our ignorance, hence giving an answer which is not "real," i.e., does not truly reflect our informed opinion. Such a person, interviewed later, could easily flip-flop to a different position, thus creating the appearance of a shift. Detecting such "noise" is important so that we do not confuse it with true change and hence bias our conclusions.

The one redeeming fact in helping identify noise is that such changes should occur at random. The people flipping in one direction should be cancelled out by the people flopping in the other. The overall pattern then will not be to create a trend but to reduce statistical relationships. We will discuss this later at greater length.

A second source of error in a panel study is what is called "mortality." During the course of a study covering several years, some people are likely to relocate, refuse reinterview, or otherwise be unavailable. In general, those who remain in the study are more likely to be socioeconomically better off, that is to say, wealthier, better educated, more socially concerned, more politically informed, more Republican. To give an example, in the second year of this study (1975) we added 348 respondents to the 451 interviewed in 1974 (of whom 280 were re-interviewed in 1975). Of the 'survivors' from 1974, 34% had incomes in excess of $20,000, while of the new 1975 group 28% had such incomes. This becomes particularly important in analyzing the 1976 vote since, by then, the surviving sample had become increasingly Republican and increasingly conservative. For that reason, analysis of the 1976 vote is based more on statistical relationships which are not dependent on sample representativeness.* Simple reporting of percent-

*To be confident in our analysis of the 1976 election, we compared 1972 and 1976 voting with the 1975 attitudes of our old *and* our new respondents. We found no significant pattern of differences in the bivariate correlations, so we were able to conclude that panel bias was not distorting the correlations in our study.

ages is used only with the 1974 and 1975 waves when the sample was more representative.

A third source of false change in a panel study is what we call "contamination," meaning that the person who has been interviewed becomes more aware and interested in politics, hence engaging in a real (but deceptive) learning process. While the learning may be good from an individual point of view it is bad from a study point of view since it is the result of being studied rather than some force at work in the society as a whole, and hence makes our panel gradually more sophisticated than the public at large. Fortunately, in our study it is a fairly small (a fraction of a point on an eight-item information scale) level, well below statistical significance. But even though small, it is not a bias for which we can easily compensate, and it is one of which we should be aware.

Estimating True Change

A typical public opinion study focuses on a set of people, a sample, taken at one point in time. In all mass data surveys the individual respondent is inevitably reduced to insignificance, but this is particularly true in the typical public opinion poll. The panel study, in contrast, is much more interested in linking specific answers to specific (though anonymous) individuals. The advantages of this approach are significant when the study focuses on changing attitudes. Imagine, for example, that for some reason in a given issue liberals were becoming more conservative and conservatives were becoming more liberal. A series of three independent public opinion studies conducted over time would not show this change, since in each case the relative balance of liberals and conservatives would remain the same. The panel, on the other hand, would immediately detect the change. In the second year it would be clear that a change was occurring, and in the third year it would be certain that it was not the result of noise.

The common technique for measuring such change is the correlation coefficient in which the answers of individuals are compared with how those individuals answered in previous years. The lower the correlation, the greater the difference in answer patterns from year to year. If random noise is the cause of change then the amount of change from wave one to wave two should be the same as the amount of change from wave one to wave three. If true changes of opinion are occurring throughout the time of our study, then there should be *more* change in the larger time period from wave one to wave three than in any shorter time span.

In our study, some questions such as party identification correlate highly with themselves over time, while others, such as whether the government should give loans to poor students, have a low correlation (see Table 4.1). The classic interpretation of low correlation is that it reflects measurement error: a bad question is being used to measure the attitude or concept. If this is true, then there are serious implications for how one would use such a measure to predict, say, voting behavior. Simply put, a question cannot be expected to correlate with another question if it does not correlate with itself. If we ask people their party identification twice and only get a correlation between the two answers of 0.7, then even if the party identification is determining voting, the correlation between voting and party will not reach 1.0, or anything above 0.7. Attitudes on issues correlate at a much lower level with themselves—around 0.3 or 0.4—and this limits their possible correlation with voting to a fairly low level. As we try to decide in the next chapter what causes people to vote, we will be faced with a problem in deciding whether partisanship or issues have the greater influence on their voting choice. The standard answer of studies such as ours is that party identification is more important than issues because it correlates much higher with the vote.

Several experts on research design cautioned us against such an approach. They said the unreliability of an item, as measured by its correlation with itself over time, puts an upper limit on how highly it can be expected to correlate with the vote. Therefore, they argue, we should make a "correction for unreliability." Thus, if government loans to poor students correlates at a .3 level with itself and, hypothetically, .3 with the vote, it would be a stronger determinant of vote than one such as party identification which correlates .7 with itself, but only, say, .5 with the vote. After all, the issue cannot correlate higher than 0.3 with vote; so one might argue that the .3 correlation shows it is determining the vote.

This is a crucial argument, for, in the example just given, accepting such a methodological position will determine the answer to the important substantive question, are voters more influenced by their party identification, or by their opinion on public issues? The specialists who advised us would "correct" the .3 correlation between attitude on loans and the vote; they would "adjust it for attentuation," thus pushing it higher than the .5 correlation between party identification and vote. They would then argue that issues are more important than party in determining vote. They would do all this on the assumption that the

TABLE 4.1
*Stability and change in attitudes**

Variable	Continuity Correlations		
	1974–75	1975–76	1974–76
1. Party identification	.70	.73	.74
2. Edward Kennedy	.58	.72	.71
3. Abortion	.60	.54	.69
4. Labor unions	.57	.69	.64
5. Reagan	.59	.54	.62
6. Wallace	.62	.62	.59
7. Democrats	.63	.64	.56
8. Capital punishment	.60	.61	.53
9. Government income	.41	.42	.52
10. Liberals	.46	.48	.50
11. Republicans	.49	.56	.49
11. Homosexuals	.50	.60	.49
11. X-rated	.43	.59	.49
11. Politicians	.44	.55	.49
15. Police search	.46	.55	.48
16. Marijuana users	.62	.53	.46
17. Big business	.42	.43	.45
17. Black employment	.40	.52	.45
17. Black militants	.47	.53	.45
20. Busing	.38	.42	.43
20. Ford	.36	.54	.43
20. Pollution	.46	.36	.43
23. Government jobs	.41	.45	.41
24. Racial intermarriage	.40	.53	.40
25. Gun control	.39	.43	.39
25. Conservatives	.46	.47	.39
27. Self-actualization	.38	—	—
27. Women's liberation	.44	.49	.38
29. Government health care	.42	.38	.37
30. Blacks	.44	.43	.35
31. Sex education	.45	.33	.34
32. Government housing	.43	.37	.32
32. Whites	.34	.42	.32
34. News bias	.49	.38	.30
35. Government education	.31	.28	.28
36. Carter	—	.06	—

*Questions arranged in order of declining two-year continuity correlations. A continuity correlation is the correlation between a variable and itself measured at two different points in time.

low correlation of an item with itself measures the unreliability of the question as it was asked.

Our basic reasoning in refusing to adopt that position is that the low correlations between an answer in 1974, 1975, and 1976 are not the result of inaccurate measurement of our respondents' opinions; they are rather a reflection of the fact that many people do not have an opinion on the question. Procedures to reach such a conclusion have been developed by Converse.[1] For example, if the low correlations were the result of unreliability, one would expect a large amount of measurement error, and high unreliability, for all respondents. Instead, Converse found that on some issues, an informed, ideological group of respondents had almost perfect correlations of their opinions across time, while another group—the less informed voters—had almost zero correlations across time. The overall .3 correlation for the sample was simply a result of the mixture of these two groups of voters. In effect, the informed had an opinion and stuck with it, while the uninformed lacked an opinion, but were embarrassed to say they did not know, and so began to give random answers. To "correct for attenuation" would be to presume that all the respondents really do have positions on various issues, and would create an artificially high causal assessment.

Patterns of Change

The correlations in Table 4.1 represent how the answers of individual respondents on specific questions compare with how those same respondents answered identical questions in different years. (Persons who did not answer a question in a given year were omitted from the analysis for that year. Similarly, questions which were not asked in two or more years could not be included.) High correlations show highly consistent responses from year to year.

In analyzing thermometer items or other items where responses fall into an ordered pattern of increasing support or opposition for a position, one should remember that the computer looks for relative position on the scale rather than specific position. That means that if there were a national trend of some sort so that every respondent moved in one direction (such as happened to Richard Nixon's popularity between 1973 and 1974) the result could still be a high correlation, since the supporters could still be supporters and opponents still opponents, even though both groups are lower on the scale.

Opinion on key political figures—Reagan, Kennedy, Wallace—are very stable over time, in some cases approaching the level of stability seen in partisanship. The image we sometimes have of wild fluctuations in politician-candidate support levels does not seem to apply to those persons who are visible to the public and known to them. While political figures have their ups and downs—Wallace, for example, dropped dramatically between 1974 and 1976—they nevertheless seem to hold their supporters and fail to impress their detractors.

On the other hand, new political figures show significant fluctuations in their support groups. Jimmy Carter, the most dramatic example, shows almost no correlation among his supporters between 1975 and 1976 when he went from an obscure southern governor to presidential candidate. Gerald Ford sprang upon the national scene in 1974 as the post-Watergate common man sent to restore integrity to the presidency. By 1975 he was no longer merely "common man" but increasingly "Republican candidate." Consequently, his supporters between 1974 and 1975 changed considerably, but between 1975 and 1976 they remained stable.[2]

Turning to partisanship, we again see noticeable stability, clear evidence that a rapid realignment was not underway. Party identification over the three-year period shows the greatest stability of any item examined in the study.[3] Other partisan related measures—Democrats, Republicans, liberals, conservatives—all show similar stability, though the redefinition of the term 'conservative' in the public mind is causing some fluctuation in that area.

In a related area, distrust of the news media seems in flux as evidenced by a significant shift from 1974 to 1976. This indicates that distrust of the news media is not a powerfully rooted attitude like party identification. Support for the media probably shifts from year to year depending on which social groups and leaders see themselves victims of media attacks. These included Nixon-Agnew supporters in 1974 (as discussed in Chapter 5), and had shifted considerably by 1976.

The New Deal dimension—the key to the present party system—shows clear evidence of stability but some *ad hoc* movement. Questions on big business, labor unions, government job programs, and government income programs reveal consistent attitudes. Clearly the New Deal is not dead (nor is opposition to it). But on specific items we see some fluctuation. Health care, government housing programs, and government education programs all reveal that a change of opinion is going on. Our suspicion is that the changes have to do with the specific programs rather than with fundamental change in the dimension. For example, in the mid 1970's, HUD scandals came very close to discrediting all federal housing programs. Likewise, the national reaction against universities in the wake of anti-war disruptions tended to weaken the credibility of those programs. On the other hand, the decisions of national unions to push for health care legislation politicized that issue to levels unseen since the 1950's. In contrast, income and jobs programs, in spite of mixed success and a diversity of programs, seemed to remain relatively stable.

All in all, the data in this table, plus the data presented in earlier chapters, seem to indicate that the old alignment continues to retain some relevance for the present era. Specific issues and specific problems create fluctuations, but the basic philosophical question—shall the government intervene to stabilize, to equalize, to compensate?— remains a matter of ongoing significance in the minds of the public. Turning to the social issue, we see a mixed pattern of change and stability. Some attitudes are clearly hardened and unchanging. Attitudes on abortion, for example, are very stable. Other attitudes such as on capital punishment, police search, black unemployment, X-rated movies, black militants, and police also show relative stability. These high correlations show the independent power of the social issue and its persistence over time. It was clearly not a temporary aberration, and could return to salience at some time in the future as it did in 1972.

Some aspects of the social issue, however, do show some fluctuation. Attitudes towards marijuana users are clearly undergoing some change, perhaps associated with the spread of usage throughout society. Women's liberation likewise is showing some change, as are attitudes on blacks and sex education in the schools. In the case of marijuana, the trend is a liberalizing one, leading to more acceptance of previously deviant groups or positions. The thermometer rating of marijuana users warms up from 25° in 1974 to 40° in 1976. It is the only social item to undergo massive net change. With so much overall stability in so great a majority of the attitudes we have studied, we do not anticipate that the divisions described will go away in the near future.

Public Response to Parties, Leaders and Issues

The social science literature records two other long term panel studies of American voters that have asked a broad battery of repeated questions. These are the 1956–1960 and 1972–1976 national election panels conducted at the Institute for Social Research, University of Michigan. Analysts have examined those studies to discover which political objects are most stable in voters' minds. For example, the 1956–1960 panel indicated that partisanship was more highly self-correlated, and hence more stable, than opinions on issues.[4] The 1972– 1976 panel indicated that opinions on political leaders ranked between partisanship and issues in terms of two-year stability.[5] Also, the 1972– 1976 panel was examined for evidence that voters had become more consistent in their opinions from year to year than they had been in the 1950's.

99

One reason it is useful to examine these differences is that high continuity correlations, are possible indicators of "attitude crystallization,"[6] and may indicate a growing degree of ideological coherence and political sophistication among voters. "Attitude crystallization" refers to the idea that if respondents think about public issues and begin to have opinions on them, they will see linkages from one issue to another that will boost correlations. With evidence from cross-sectional surveys, Nie has argued that American voters have organized their political attitudes into more highly inter-correlated clusters than in earlier decades.[7]

Converse and Markus address this problem with the help of the 1972–1976 national panel study. Issue continuity correlations, they found, were much more variable in the 1972–1976 panel than in the 1956–1960 study. In particular, some "moral" issues such as abortion had very high continuity correlations in the 1970's, but other issues showed the pattern of lower continuity correlations typical in the 1950's.[8] Table 4.2 shows the degree of overlap of questions between our study and theirs.[9] Our analysis can enrich their findings in at least two ways. First, because we asked many questions identical to the ones asked in the national panel and also many unique questions, we can use the continuity correlations from the former to demonstrate the similarity of Dearborn to the nation, and then use the continuity correlations from the latter to extend our understanding into new areas. Second, we can apply the Alignment and Disintegration framework from chapter three to help resolve the problem of what *types* of issues have the high continuity correlations that have aroused such interest.

Our technique is to classify questions according to the factor structure of chapter three, and to rank the questions from the highest continuity correlations to the lowest. The continuity correlations over a two-year span were used to insure maximum comparability to the I.S.R. studies. Each dimension of public opinion can then be compared to the others to see which is the most stable. One way to compare the dimensions is in order of the highest continuity correlation each one contains. Thus, Partisanship would rank first because one of its elements, party identification, has the highest continuity correlation (.74); opinions on political leaders would rank second because the Edward Kennedy thermometer has a continuity correlation of .71; and New Morality would rank third because abortion attitudes have a continuity correlation of .69. Another approach would be to rank the dimensions in terms of the average continuity correlation for all the items within each dimension. The first approach runs the risk of in-

TABLE 4.2
Overlap between Dearborn three-wave panel opinion questions
(N = 45) and the Michigan CPS three-wave questions

In CPS Study With Same Wording (N = 13):	Not in CPS Three Waves (N = 25)*
Liberals	Homosexuals
Policemen	Politicians
Democrats	Ronald Reagan
Whites	Gerald Ford
Labor unions	News bias
Black militants	Taxes to reduce pollution
Republicans	Black unemployment
Blacks	Racial intermarriage
Conservatives	Sex education
Edward Kennedy	X-rated films
George Wallace	Happiness now
Public officials don't	Happiness in future
care	Happiness five years ago
Politics so complicated	Parties don't care
	Can't do anything about public
With Slightly	affairs
Different Wording	Politicians can be trusted
(N = 7):	Government housing loans
	Government student loans
Big business	Capital punishment
Women's liberation movement	Police search
Marijuana users	
Nation's problems (Open)	Abortion
Busing	Government health care
Don't have much say	Government jobs
Party identification	Government income
	maintenance

*Most of the items in this column have no counterparts at all in the CPS panel; examples would be the questions on Ronald Reagan, taxes to reduce pollution, and personal happiness. Some items, however, do tap issues that are examined in the CPS panel. Abortion, for example, is in the CPS study; one CPS seven-point scale on government medical insurance and another combining government income and job guarantees are similar to some of our New Deal panel items. Thus, a few items at the end of the right hand column might be reclassified to a category C in the left hand column: "too different in coding and wording to be easily compared across the studies, but attempting to measure the same attitude."

stability because it stakes everything on one correlation; the second approach runs the danger of diminishing a factor because a few confusing or poorly worded questions, with consequently low continuity correlations, were included in it. Neither approach is clearly superior; fortunately, they both produce about the same results.

As seen in Table 4.3, Partisanship has the highest stability (with continuity correlations ranking from 1st to 11th in stability). Next comes attitudes toward political leaders (continuity correlations rank-

101

ing from 2nd to 20th). Then come New Morality items (continuity correlations from 3rd to 31st), the single Racial Fears item (continuity correlation ranking 17th), and the Law and Order items (continuity correlations from 8th to 25th). New Deal is lower (continuity correlations from 9th to 34th). In other words, three of the cross-cutting dimensions are more stable than the New Deal issues that ostensibly created and sustain the party system. Furthermore, the type of instability for the New Deal issues indicates voter confusion and random responses, whereas the instability that does exist on New Morality is partly a consequence of people genuinely changing their minds. This can be seen (in Table 4.1) in the continuity correlations on women's liberation, marijuana, and perhaps sex education, where the time one to time three continuity correlations are much lower than the time one to time two or time two to time three continuity correlations. Hence, the New Morality, Racial Fear, and Law and Order dimensions not only tend to be more stable than New Deal, but also seem to have a higher ratio of purposive to random change.

But not all dimensions of the Disintegration Cluster possess the relatively stable continuity correlations of the New Morality, Racial Fears, and Law and Order. Racial Prejudice and the Inglehart value hierarchy have continuity correlations as weak as New Deal. It seems that Racial Prejudice, most salient in national politics from 1954 to the mid-1960's, exhibits the low continuity correlations that one associates with issues, such as New Deal, from the 1950's and before.

Since the "new issues" of the Disintegration Cluster—Law and Order and the New Morality—are accounting for the highest continuity correlations among issue items, it would appear that much of the increased stability of political beliefs from the 1950's to the 1970's is not the result of increased education of the populace, nor an across-the-board effect of leadership. Rather, it seems linked to the emergence of highly emotional cross-cutting issues—New Morality, Law and Order, and Racial Fear—that produced stronger and more persistent opinions among the electorate than had been true of the issues that dominated political debate in the 1950's and early 1960's.

These debates about issues, leaders, and parties should not distract from other important findings in Table 4.3. Some of the unclassified political objects in the last column of the table merit our attention because of their high stability. Most notably, the attitude towards labor unions is the fourth highest continuity correlation in the entire table. Labor unions rank up with the most stable national political figures—Kennedy, Reagan, and Wallace—and the most stable issue—abortion.

TABLE 4.3
Stability of each type of issue, and of other opinions, 1974–1976*

Party	Political Leaders	New Morality	Law & Order	Racial Fears	New Deal	Racial Prejudice	Inglehart Values	Miscellaneous
1	2							
		3						4 (Unions)
	5							
	6							
7		8			9			
								10 (Liberals)
11	11	11,11						
		16	15					
				17		17		17 (Business)
	20		20					20 (Pollution)
					23	24		
		27	25					25 (Conservatives)
					29	30	27**	
		31			32	32		
					35			34 (News Bias)
Mean= 6.3	Mean= 8.8	Mean= 16.5	Mean= 17.0	Mean= 17.0	Mean= 25.6	Mean= 25.8	Mean= 27.0	Mean= 18.3

*The numbers in this table are the rankings of the continuity correlations from Table 4.1.

**The Inglehart dimension is measured with a one-year continuity correlation coefficient because the same question was not repeated in three consecutive years.

Indeed, labor unions (a thermometer item) rank ahead of Democrats and Republicans (two other thermometer items, and hence more directly comparable than party identification) in stability as a political object. Not far below labor unions, liberals rank 10th in stability—an intriguing finding that indicates that the vague ideological phrase, "liberal," is beginning to become an anchored point of reference in the minds of many voters. Big business and conservatives seem to have a less stable following and opposition. At least in the case of big business, this seems to be because many random changes of opinion are occurring. (Note, in Table 4.1, that the T_1 to T_3 continuity correlation is of the same magnitude as the T_1 to T_2 and the T_2 to T_3 continuity correlations.) The lowest correlation among the miscellaneous political objects is that for the bias attributed to news media. Opinions on media bias show signs of high volatility. Perhaps a person's opinion about media bias reflects the person's respect for the current targets of media criticism. This would explain why, over a two-year period, opinions on the media undergo massive turnover, as the media shift their attention from institution to institution and from former President to new incumbent.

In conclusion, the high stability of party identification suggests strongly that no rapid realignment was occurring during the years of our study. The high stability of attitudes on Law and Order, Racial Fears, and New Morality, however, suggest that the Disintegration Cluster has considerable staying power and the potential to disrupt future elections in which it might become salient. This opens the stage for our examination of the 1972 and 1976 presidential elections, which seem to have been significantly affected by shifts in issue saliency. This feature, and other aspects of these two elections, are the concern of the next chapter.

CHAPTER 5: The Presidential Elections of 1972 and 1976

In analyzing an election, political scientists sometimes find it helpful to distinguish between long term and short term forces.[1] Long term forces consist primarily of two factors: individual identification with parties, and major policy (or ideological) divisions between the parties. These factors tend to be very stable over time. Once a voter develops an identification with a party, that identification usually persists from election to election; once parties have taken positions on controversial issues, or have staked out ideological positions, they seldom change those positions in any but marginal, incremental ways. Add to this the fact that public opinion on key issues tends to be fairly stable (though less so on details of how to implement policies), and we realize that the presence and persistence of long range factors leads to a remarkable stability in electoral systems. This stability is best seen in elections for the House of Representatives where, more than anywhere else, voters tend to follow long run patterns. These long run patterns are so persistent that political scientists have developed the concept of a "normal" vote. A normal vote is the vote which Democrats and Republicans would get in a national race in which all patterns of behavior were statistically what one would predict based upon regular known patterns of behavior. If everything came out in a "normal" way, during the period of our panel study, the Democrats should have gotten 54% of the national vote and the Republicans 46%.[2]

But clearly Democrats do not win all national elections, and even when the Republicans lose they seldom lose by such landslide margins as 54–46. To explain why this is so, we must turn to the second set of factors which go into any election—short term elements.

105

A short term factor is one which is important only for that one election. It does not persist over time, and does not have an impact upon the long-range division of power between the parties. It does not induce Democrats to become Republicans or Republicans to become Democrats. It can, however, induce an identifying Democrat or an identifying Republican to temporarily abandon his party to vote for the opposition candidate.

Short term factors come in several forms: an issue which rises to sudden prominence (such as the matter of amnesty for war resisters and draft evaders in 1972) but later fades; a scandal in administration; the nomination of a candidate who is personally unattractive, or attractive; a foreign policy setback or triumph; feelings that a given candidate is eminently qualified or capable, or the opposite. All of these can and do seduce voters away from their regular party into the arms of the opposition, but without inducing any permanent change in the political system.

To analyze any given election then, one must ask several questions about the configuration of issues at the time. Most important is the question of whether party identifications remain strong. If the majority party is able to activate party identifications so as to encourage a party vote, then the Democrats will always defeat the Republicans in a national race. Since World War II, however, only 1948 (Truman-Dewey) and 1960 (Kennedy-Nixon) have been considered "party elections". In all other years, there have been major deviations from predicted party patterns.

Tied in closely with the stability of party vote is the extent to which the long range policy or ideological positions which divide the parties are salient and persistent. Democrats and Republicans are historically (since 1932) at odds on what we call "New Deal" issues, specifically, the extent to which the federal government should provide aid programs for the helpless, provide cushions for the temporarily displaced, provide subsidized programs (education, job training) for the deprived, and regulate private enterprise to insure stability and growth, availability of jobs, and a more equitable division of wealth. Thus, if the electorate is worried about unemployment, unfair taxes, or rising medical costs, the Democrats will have a natural advantage, for on these issues the majority of the public prefers a Democratic position. If, on the other hand, these issues are not important, or if the Democrats are seen as being temporarily inefficient in implementing their policies, the advantage of the Democrats could be neutralized.

A third factor to consider is whether there is a surging "new issue" which has taken over the headlines. An issue such as crime, an unpopular war, a public scandal, or social conflict can split a party and produce an unexpected result. The new issues on which we have focused our attention in this work—law and order, life styles, and race—were all prominent in 1972, when they seemed to unite the Republicans on the right, and split the Democrats into conservative and liberal wings. The question in 1976 was whether they were still important.

A final matter to keep in mind is the candidates themselves. A popular candidate can strengthen his party just as an unpopular one can weaken it. Personal attractiveness, experience, and the ability to inspire confidence are all elements which influence the ultimate vote of individuals.

In our analysis of the elections of 1972 and 1976, and the events between, we would like to suggest that several major short term and long term processes were at work:

1. In 1972 the salience of the New Deal/economic cluster declined, depriving the Democrats of a natural issue advantage. This occurred primarily because of the expansionist policies of Nixon's Secretary of the Treasury, John Connally. Connally's policies produced a temporary prosperity which did not give way to recession and inflation until 1974.

2. At the same time, the salience of the new issues increased, thus polarizing the Democratic party and giving the more united Republicans a temporary short term victory. With the economic issue temporarily neutralized, the Republicans succeeded in dramatizing the presidential campaign as a symbolic contest between two different cultures: the radicals who favored protest and change versus the silent majority who favored law and order and prosperity.

3. Short term party image and candidate qualities ran in favor of the Republicans, thus giving them a further advantage. We do not have data on these dimensions since our first interviews were collected in 1974. However, the trend is well documented in other research, as well as the public opinion polls of the day.[3]

4. Any gains which the Republicans might have achieved in 1972 were nullified by 1974, when the Watergate scandal reached its peak. Our data show that the defecting Democrats of 1972 were most affected by that scandal. Watergate induced no realignment, but played a major role in restoring the previous alignment, which was heavily in favor of the Democrats.

5. The economic decline, which began in 1973, was accelerated by the oil crisis of October 1974. By the end of 1974, the image of Rich-

ard Nixon as a financial wizard had become a thing of the past.[4] With unemployment, double-digit inflation, and long lines at gas stations, wavering Democrats began once again to perceive the Republican party as the party of financial disaster, and to look at their Democratic roots for salvation. By 1976 the New Deal cleavage had re-emerged. The salience of economic-social welfare issues tended to reactivate partisan patterns and to shift the advantage back to the majority Democratic party.

6. At the same time issues such as race and crime temporarily declined in relative salience, thus enabling Democratic identifiers to return to their party. Part of this neutralization of social issues was due to the rise of Jimmy Carter, who was perceived as a moderate on most of the life style, race relations, law and order, and protest and change issues that had fractured Democratic ranks.

We want to emphasize that party identification remained solid even in 1972, and the Democratic vote for Congress remained firm. Because of the emergence of new issues in the 1960's, however, voters had developed the habit of ticket splitting.[5] But because such defectors remained Democratic identifiers, Carter was able to mobilize them in 1976. By the time of the presidential election in November of that year, partisanship had become so important that party identification emerges as a major predictor of presidential vote. Issues were largely irrelevant to that prediction, and the voter's opinion of the character and capability of the candidates—opinions largely shaped by party identification—were the only significant predictors of votes besides party identification.

The 1972 Election

The 1972 Presidential election was characterized by massive defections of Democrats into the Nixon camp. In our study, for example, 42% of the Democrats voted for Nixon, and only 58% for their own nominee, McGovern (the national pattern was identical).[6] In this section we will show that this defection was strongly related to the conservatism of these Democrats on life style, law and order, and racial issues. A cross-cutting cleavage had struck the party system and split the Democratic vote in half.

A comparison of these issues with 1972 vote patterns shows a fracture of the Democratic Party on most new issues. Democrats who voted for Nixon are not only more conservative than McGovern

Democrats, but they are even more conservative than Nixon Republicans. In many ways the Democratic party is a coalition of diverse viewpoints, representing the whole political spectrum, from far left to far right. The Republican party, in contrast, is much more ideologically cohesive. The emergence of the new issues as politically salient topics split the Democratic right away from the party and drove them to seek allies among Republicans. The critical consideration, of course, is not whether your allies exactly replicate your own views, but rather how close they are to your views when compared with other possible allies. What we have found in the case of the 1972 election is that in each of the new issues, the defecting Democrats are closer to the Republicans than they are to loyalist Democrats, when we compare percentages of the group taking a certain position.[7] Of the issues to be discussed below, the distances between the relevant groups are as follows:

TABLE 5.1.
Distances between voting groups on major issues (percentage)

Issue Dimension	Gap between McGovern Democrats and Nixon Democrats	Gap between Nixon Republicans and Nixon Democrats
Law and order	25	3.5
Racial fears	27	11.0
Life style	16	8.0
Prejudice	10	6.0

Law and Order: We measured the Law and Order component of the new cross-cutting cleavage with an index of three items: a conservative point was given for support of the death penalty, and for agreement with the statements, "Judges are too soft on criminals" and "Police should have a right to search a suspicious person without worrying about his rights." Voters with two or three points on the index were called conservative, those with zero or one point, liberal. Even the McGovern Democrats were predominantly conservative on this index, but they were more than twice as liberal as any other identifiable vote group. It was these liberals whom Richard Nixon attacked in 1968 and 1972 in order to induce the defection of other Democrats. As Table 5.2 shows, the Democratic camp was split on this issue, with some Democrats more liberal and some more conservative than the Republicans. By and large the conservative Democrats defected and joined the Nixon camp.

TABLE 5.2
Voting patterns and issue position in 1972 (% conservative)

Issue Dimension	McGovern Democrats	Nixon Independents	Nixon Republicans	Nixon Democrats	χ^2 Significance
		Voting Group			
Law and order	64.5	84.6	85.9	89.4	.001
Racial fears (High)	60.5	73.7	76.8	87.8	.005
Life style	70.4	62.5	77.9	86.0	.09
Racial prejudice	14.1	17.6	18.4	24.5	.53

Racial Fears: We constructed an index of Racial Fear by giving a person one point if he rated black militants below 20°, one point if he rated urban rioters below 20°, and one point if he was strongly opposed to busing. Again, a score of two or three was conservative, zero or one, liberal. Just as on the law and order items, the Democrats split on the index of Racial Fears and again we see that the defecting Democrats are more conservative on this issue than the Republicans they joined.

Sex and Life Style: The Life Style Index—composed of support for abortion, warm feelings towards homosexuals, support for sex education and showing X-rated films—was also related to the Democratic defection, but the pattern fell just short of statistical significance. (Scores of zero to two were liberal, three and four, conservative.) The Nixon Democrats were the most conservative group, but in this case the McGovern Democrats were not the most liberal—the independents were.

Racial Prejudice: Our five-point Racial Prejudice Index was constructed by giving a point for cold feelings toward blacks, blaming black people for the black unemployment rate, disapproval or moral condemnation of interracial marriage, and advising blacks to be patient, work harder, stop rioting or obey the law. A conservative was someone who had four or more points. The Racial Prejudice dimension was not significantly related to the voting patterns, though the Nixon Democrats were, by an insignificant amount, the most prejudiced group. Again, we see evidence that the disruption occurring in the political system was more complex than simple racial prejudice.

New Deal: The key long range issue dividing the parties relates to the role of the federal government in the economy. As was discussed earlier, when this issue is salient, the Democrats have a natural advan-

110

TABLE 5.3
The New Deal dimension (% liberal)

McGovern Democrats	Nixon Democrats	Nixon Independents	Nixon Republicans
74.0	68.8	51.4	29.9

χ^2 Significance is .001 for the table as a whole; difference between McGovern Democrats and Nixon Democrats is not significant at .05 level.

tage, since there is a liberal majority in the country. Phillips, among others, suggested that the Democratic Party was polarized on this issue.[8] Our data show otherwise. The New Deal index (Table 5.3) indicates the unity of all Democrats. (On this index, zero through two is a conservative response, three or more is a liberal one.)

Nixon Democrats are not fundamentally different from McGovern Democrats. It is clear that the 1972 election did not polarize the Democratic party on this dimension. On the contrary, it must have been irrelevant to most voters for it seemed to make so little difference. Moreover, when we compare Democrats with Republicans we do find differences. Clearly, the New Deal dimension was as alive and well as it was in the past when it contributed to such Democratic dominance of the political sphere. The fact that it remained strong also created the potential for its re-emergence in 1976 if the issue concerns of the populace were relevant.

Predicting the 1972 Vote*

The evidence presented above shows how a series of attitudes are associated with the 1972 vote. Such evidence is called "bivariate" because it shows how one variable (or set of variables viewed together) such as voting for McGovern, is related to a second attitude or set of attitudes, such as believing that the government should make sure everyone has a good standard of living. Such evidence is limited because it leaves out other relevant variables by focusing on only two. One problem this creates is that it is impossible to know what is causing the correlation between the two variables. In the example above, a

*Note that "prediction" in this sense does not mean looking into the future but is rather a statistical term which refers to the measurement of correct guesses based on a theory. While we as observers know who won the 1972 and 1976 elections the computer in a sense does not; hence we are able to get computer "predictions" of the outcome, which we can compare with actual voting patterns.

111

person may well have voted for McGovern *because* he believes that the government ought to make sure everyone has a decent standard of living. However, in some cases of association a correlation may be "spurious"—that is, one which only appears to be causal. A third variable, related to the two we are examining, may be the true cause. For example, people may vote for McGovern *because they are Democrats*. If Democrats have grown up believing in government income-maintenance programs, there may then be a correlation between attitudes on government income-maintenance and voting for McGovern. In fact, voters may not even know McGovern's position on income maintenance, but because issue position is associated with party identification the researcher who studies only issues without looking at party identification will think issue position is what is causing the vote.

"Multivariate" evidence—involving more than two variables—can solve this problem of causality for us if we correctly specify what all the relevant variables are. We can then move from saying what correlates with people's vote to saying what causes people's vote. A further advantage of multivariate analysis is that, when we look at all the relevant variables at once, we can know what percentage of votes we have successfully predicted from knowing what we do about political opinions. Moreover, we can say exactly how important each variable is compared to the others in our prediction.

In this analysis we have two different types of multivariate statistics: Path analysis and discriminant analysis (to be explained shortly). We used two techniques to double-check the results. Each method makes assumptions about data which may not be exactly true in our study. In fact, the results are very similar, regardless of the particular statistic and assumption used.[9]

The model we use to explain the 1972 vote is presented in Figure 5.1. A model, of course, is just a graphic or conceptual depiction of relationships. In our model, the arrows represent the ways in which we believe one variable is causing another. We believe that a person's vote for Nixon or McGovern is largely caused by that person's party identification, his evaluation of the candidates (as measured by thermometers on the two men), and his position on key issues. These issues, as discussed in chapter three, we divide into New Deal social welfare items on the one hand and cross-cutting issues (post-materialism, law and order, race, and life style) on the other. We believe that post-materialism is a basic value that causes people to hold specific attitudes on law and order and life style issues. The evaluation of candidates is itself in part the product of the person's party identifica-

112

Figure 5.1 A Model of the 1972 Election

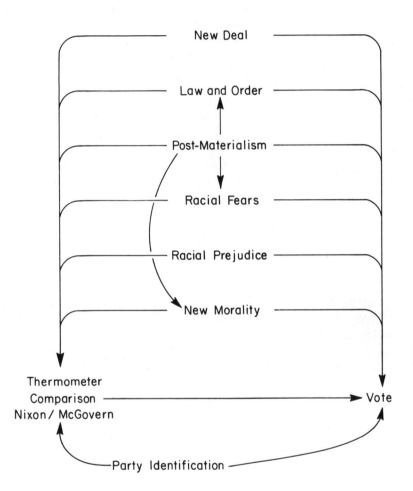

tion (a Republican will tend to like Nixon) and issue position (a conservative will tend to like Nixon). The evaluation of candidates is thus an "intervening variable," that is, it is caused by one set of variables (party identification and issue position) and causes another (the vote). Hence, the arrows in the model—which represent "causal paths"—run in two directions in some cases. Path analysis produces numbers that measure the strength of each causal path. The variable at the begin-

113

ning of a path is called "independent," and the one at the end is called "dependent," since its value depends on the independent variables. The numbers that measure the strength of each causal path vary from zero, when the causal impact is zero, to one, when the dependent variable is totally dominated by the independent variable (an impossibility since human attitudes are too complex to be fully explained). An independent variable, like party identification, can have both direct effects, through its path directly to vote, and indirect effects, by influencing an intervening variable like candidate evaluation, which in turn causes the vote. Discriminant analysis, in contrast, tells us the percentage of dependent variable responses we can correctly guess or predict if we know, in advance, responses or positions on a given independent variable. Interpretation of discriminant analysis is easy since it generates for us a simple percentage figure—what percentage of the votes have been correctly predicted. The statistics generated by path analysis are slightly more complex since they indicate the relative importance of each of the causes of the vote.

Analyzing the Results

As seen in Table 5.4 and Figure 5.2, party identification (even in a year of massive defection) is the dominant predictor of the 1972 vote. It has strong direct impact on the vote and even more powerful influence on the voters' evaluation of the candidates. Candidate evaluation—comparing McGovern and Nixon—had the strongest direct impact on the vote. Some of the cross-cutting issues also affected the election significantly.

We included in our path analyses all 25 variables from the factor analysis of chapter three (see Table 3.1). One item at a time from each factor was tested until we had the combination of issue items that explained the most variance in the vote. By this inductive procedure, issue factors were eliminated from the path analysis if none of their variables explained a significant (.05 level) amount of the variance in voting. We were left with a few variables that were significant, and each of these was used as an indicator of the factor on which it had its highest loading.

We chose this procedure rather than the use of factor scores or multi-item indices because in such procedures the sample becomes biased and many cases are lost because of missing data.*

*Alternative procedures were tried, with results roughly similar to those reported in Figure 5.3. For example, multi-item indices, measuring each of the six issue and value

TABLE 5.4
Relative importance of variables in predicting the 1972 vote. (path analysis)

Variable	Effects		
	Direct	Indirect	Total
Party identification	.33	.20	.53
Candidate Thermometer difference (measured in 1974)	.40	N.A.	.40
Women's liberation	.09	.06	.15
Busing	.10	.00	.10
Post-materialism	.09	.01	.10

In the path diagrams for both 1972 and 1976, we have not drawn any causal linkages between party identification and New Deal issues. We believe that there is some reciprocal causation between party identification and attitudes on New Deal issues, but we do not have the data to test which direction is the more important in this relationship, and we treat the correlation between those two items as an unanalyzed correlation between exogenous variables. As for the Disintegration Cluster of five cross-cutting issues, we do not believe that partisanship had a significant impact on attitude formation on these issues. When we began our study, we anticipated that these issues might cause partisan change in the form of realignment, and we have tested for this relationship, but found no significant impact. Women's liberation—our indicator of the Life Style dimension—had the strongest effect on the vote of all the issues we examined. Busing and post-materialism also played a significant role. None of the racial fears or racial prejudice questions was significantly related to the vote, but in the case of racial fears this may be because busing has a racial fears as well as a law and order component. An important question, of course, is the percentage of the respondent's votes we can correctly predict when we know party identification, thermometer comparisons, and positions on key issues (in this case busing, women's liberation, and post-materialism).[10] Using

---

dimensions from Table 3.1, were used in place of the single items. The indices were constructed by coding each voter as liberal or conservative on the items in Table 3.1. A regression analysis including index scores, plus party identification and candidate thermometer differences, was used to predict the vote. The results are comparable. The R^2 is .52 (N = 222). Each index has an effect on the vote, in the predicted direction, but only three of the effects are significant (at the .05 level). The significant beta coefficients are those for the candidate thermometer comparison ($-.36$), party identification ($-.29$), and Post-Materialism (.14). The vote may still be interpreted as a product of candidate evaluation, partisanship, and the impact of forces from the Disintegration Cluster.

Figure 5.2 The 1972 Vote (Path Analysis) **

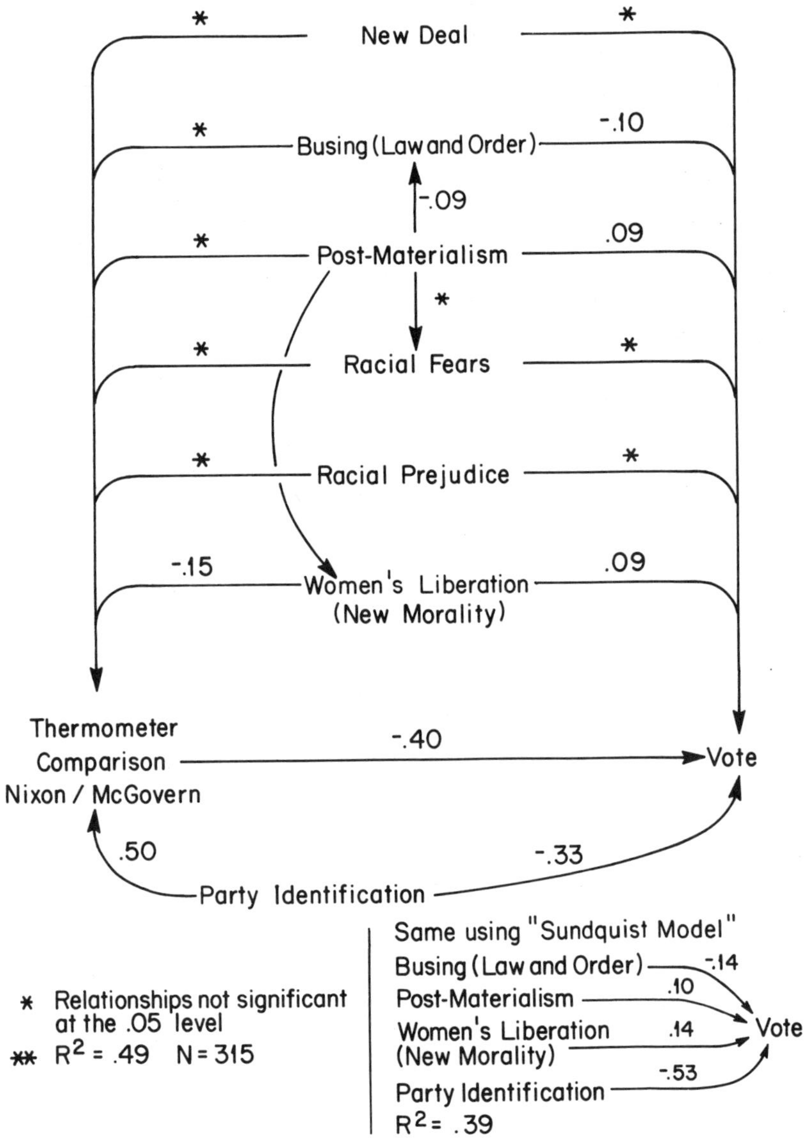
*
New Deal
*
*
Busing (Law and Order)
-.10
-.09
*
Post-Materialism
.09
*
*
Racial Fears
*
*
Racial Prejudice
*
-.15
Women's Liberation
(New Morality)
.09
Thermometer
Comparison
Nixon / McGovern
-.40
Vote
.50
-.33
Party Identification
Same using "Sundquist Model"
Busing (Law and Order)
-.14
Post-Materialism
.10
Women's Liberation
(New Morality)
.14
Vote
-.53
Party Identification
R2= .39

* Relationships not significant at the .05 level

** R^2 = .49 N = 315

discriminant analysis, a technique designed to answer that question, we can correctly predict 91% of the McGovern voters and 83% of the Nixon voters. Thus, except for the thermometer evaluation of the candidates, the variables that explain the 1972 election are variables from our model of party realignment; namely, existing party identification and new cross-cutting issues.[11] Even the thermometer comparison of the candidates, because it is affected by party identification and the candidates' stands on the cross-cutting issues, is related indirectly to the party realignment model. An interesting question, though, is how well we can predict the election if we limit ourselves to variables directly in our realignment model, and exclude candidate thermometer comparisons. The answer (measured by R^2, the percentage of variance explained) is that we account for 80% of the voting decisions we could predict when we had candidate comparisons to help us. Thus, our party realignment model remains the heart of any explanation of the 1972 vote. Cross-cutting issues disrupted voting patterns just as the realignment framework would predict. However, voters were ticket splitting and keeping their old party identification, rather than realigning. A problem for realignment theory is to explain why ticket splitting, rather than realignment, was occurring. We have provided one possible explanation at the start of this chapter, but will return to this question later.

Response to Watergate

The Watergate scandal was the major political issue of the four years between the 1972 and the 1976 presidential elections. Watergate ended the Nixon presidency in disgrace, put Gerald Ford in the White House, and set the stage for the 1976 contest between Ford and Jimmy Carter, a political outsider whose plea for a political system "as decent as the American people themselves" had definite Watergate-related overtones.

Our basic thesis about the impact of Watergate on party alignments is that the whole affair tended to reinforce traditional partisan patterns and to reverse or seriously modify any tendency to realignment which might have been occurring among Democrats who had defected in 1972. Testing this thesis is not easy, but we do have certain evidence which lends support to it. What we would like to suggest is that Watergate induced an abandonment of the Nixon administration, not by all Americans, but by certain types of Americans, and that the rate of that abandonment and the public response to the whole affair was primarily structured by pre-Watergate identifications and behavior patterns, particularly those emanating from the 1972 presidential election. In that election, millions of voters were convinced that the choice between the two main candidates was a clear one, and that Richard Nixon was the one to choose. In unprecedented numbers, Democrats defected to the opposition, and with unprecedented unanimity, Republicans rallied to their nominee. In many ways, it was one of the most polarizing elections in years, with many bitter feelings on both sides. People decided early whom they were going to support, and the public opinion polls evidenced little change in the last weeks of campaigning.[12]

Following the election and inauguration, as it became obvious that Watergate was not going to go away, evidence of administration wrong-doing increased. Talk of wheat deals, milk deals, illegal loans, cover-ups, suppression of evidence, bribes, illegal campaign contributions, perjury, tax evasion, and presidential involvement began to seem more credible, even to Nixon supporters. Doubt began to creep in where conviction had once stood. The president went on television but seemed to many to be unconvincing. The Ervin committee paraded many of the accused on national television, Archibald Cox was fired, and Elliot Richardson resigned. Spiro Agnew pleaded no contest to tax evasion charges and left office. Prominent Republicans like Senator Barry Goldwater publicly criticized the president's handling of the charges.[13]

If these developments vindicated the beliefs of many McGovern Democrats, they were deeply disturbing to those who identified with the Republican Party and those who had voted for Richard Nixon in 1972. The initial reaction of many of the latter was disbelief. In early April, 1973, the Gallup Poll showed that a full 53% of the public felt that the Watergate matter was "just politics."[14] Supporters of the president insisted that he himself had known nothing of what was happening, that his accusers were lying, that the news media were out to get him, that the accusations were part of a partisan effort by Democrats to discredit his administration, and that Presidents Kennedy and Johnson had done even worse things while they were in office.

As the mass of evidence against the president began to build up, many of his supporters gave up and abandoned the administration. The president's popularity dropped from 68% to 31% in just seven months. His supporters became less vocal and fewer in number. By early 1974 when we did our first wave of interviews, potentially incriminating evidence had been brought out by investigative reporters

118

TABLE 5.5
Ordering of commitment to Nixon administration

Commitment Type	Points Assigned	Rank Order of Commitment	N
Nixon Republican	+2	1	99
Nixon Independent	+1	2	39
Nixon Democrat	0	3	70
McGovern Democrat	−2	4	95

Other combinations, particularly McGovern Republicans and McGovern independents, comprised a miniscule portion of the sample, and consequently were omitted from the analysis.

and Senator Ervin's senate committee. While this evidence had not yet prompted the convening of the House Judiciary Committee's impeachment hearing, Nixon's support base had been reduced to a fraction of its original size. We will attempt to show who these hard core supporters were in terms of previous support groups. In particular, we will examine the interaction of two factors, partisan identification, and vote in 1972, as components of a framework which structured response to the Watergate issue. We will attempt to show how this framework shaped perception of three main personalities—President Nixon, former Vice-President Spiro Agnew, and Senator Sam Ervin, head of the Senate Watergate Committee. We will also show how this framework influenced the priority placed upon Watergate as an issue in the political system.

We used two measures with which we imputed a prior level of commitment to the Nixon administration: party identification and 1972 presidential vote. For identifying with the Republican party and voting the Nixon-Agnew ticket in 1972 we assigned one point each, giving a Nixon Republican a total of two points. For identifying with the Democratic party or voting the McGovern-Shriver ticket in 1972, we assigned minus one point each, giving a McGovern Democrat a total of minus two points. For identifying as an independent, we gave zero points, meaning that a Nixon independent would have a score of one point. This gave us the following commitment-level ordering.

Our procedure for assessing Watergate attitudes was twofold: first, measure the extent to which Watergate was perceived as a major national problem and, second, analyze the thermometer scores of three major personalities in the conflict: President Nixon, former Vice-President Spiro Agnew, and Senator Sam Ervin. As Table 5.6 shows, Senator Ervin's mean score was the highest of the three. The only politician to surpass him was Gerald Ford, vice-president at the time of the survey. Of the eight politicians and 21 political and social groups tested in 1974, Agnew's mean score was one of only four below 30° (the other three, ironically, were urban rioters, black militants, and marijuana users). No other political figure was anywhere near that low. Nixon's score, likewise low when compared with other political figures, also shows a very high standard deviation, indicating a wide range of opinion on him. It is the nature of this range of opinion which is the focus of the analysis.

Commitment to Nixon

We had several patterns which we expected to emerge if our basic logic was correct. To begin with, those few people who still supported President Nixon in 1974 would be concentrated mostly at the top of the commitment scale. Second, we expected that the commitment framework would also predict well to the Ervin thermometer.

Ervin, as chairman of the Senate Watergate Committee, was the symbol of righteous indignation in the face of the "White House horrors." It was he who laid bare the extent of what had happened; he who forced expressions of shame from Nixon confidants; he who, on live television, reminded the nation that, "God is not mocked, for whatsoever a man soweth, that also shall he reap." It was he whose credibility must be discounted if one were to maintain one's faith in the president. We suspected that the committed person would perceive Ervin as a shrewd partisan, a "stalking horse for the Kennedys," an already committed enemy of the Nixon administration, and hence would rate him low.

We also expected that the commitment structure would predict well to the level of concern about the Watergate issue. Respondents were asked to name what they thought was the single most important problem facing this country, and then to name the second most important problem. In this open-ended question, 26% mentioned corruption in government or Watergate as the number one national problem, and an additional 21% mentioned it as the second most important problem. In this way we split our sample into roughly half who expressed serious concern about Watergate and about half who were more concerned about other problems. The Watergate-concerned person had singled out this topic as more important than race-relations, crime, inflation, unemployment, or taxes. We expected that McGovern Democrats would be most likely to do so, and that Nixon Republicans, who had

TABLE 5.6
Thermometer scores of
Watergate-related personalities

	Mean	Standard Deviation
Sam Ervin	58.5	22.5
Richard M. Nixon	41.2	31.0
Spiro Agnew	28.3	25.6

TABLE 5.7
Thermometer score ranges

	0–30	31–70	71–100
Sam Ervin	12.8%	63.0%	24.2%
Richard M. Nixon	40.3%	44.4%	15.3%
Spiro Agnew	58.6%	37.0%	4.4%

committed part of their identity to the Nixon cause, would be least likely.

The national news media also played a role in Watergate. Almost since its first inauguration in January, 1969, the Nixon administration had made an effort to portray the media as a front-group for leftist-liberal-Democratic causes.[15] Former Vice-President Agnew in particular spoke on this theme many times. Television correspondents were singled out for investigation and attack by administration officials. The media were accused of distorting the news, sensationalizing it, rumor-mongering, and even fabricating lies. We expected that individuals committed to the administration would be aware of the wide coverage given by the media to the Watergate scandal and would compensate by questioning the credibility of the reporting itself. An individual who receives contradictory information about a person or object feels a sense of uneasiness or dissonance.[16] The Nixon administration tried to reduce dissonance (and thus increase their credibility) by discrediting the national media. It was our expectation that perception of media fault would closely correlate with the commitment measure, also an indicator of dissonance.*

In general, most of these expectations are proven to be true, but with some interesting variations. To start with, we found a close rela-

---

*It should be noted that we are measuring commitment and inferring dissonance. We do not have a direct measure of cognitive dissonance.

TABLE 5.8
*Feeling toward Watergate personalities, by commitment level**

Commitment Type:	Commitment Level:	Anti-Administration Feelings: Percentage Ranking . . .		
		Ervin Higher than 70	Agnew Lower than 20	Nixon Lower than 30
McGovern Democrats	4	40%	68%	60%
Nixon Democrats	3	28%	46%	24%
Nixon Independents	2	13%	44%	20%
Nixon Republicans	1	7%	30%	9%

*Agnew is analyzed in terms of an 80–20 breakdown because of the concentration of opinions at the lower range of the scale.
χ^2 significance = .0000

tionship between the commitment measure and attitudes toward Nixon, Agnew, and Ervin. This finding is perhaps not surprising or even insightful in the cases of Nixon and Agnew, but it does provide some opportunity for intelligent hypothesizing in the case of Ervin. Unlike Nixon and Agnew, Senator Ervin is a post-Watergate personality who was essentially unknown outside the limited circles before the creation of the Senate Watergate Committee. If attitudes toward Ervin follow the same pattern as attitudes toward Nixon and Agnew, then we have been able to predict from one configuration of behavior to a new attitude situation.

The actual pattern is seen in Table 5.8. The data suggest that respondents formed evaluations of Ervin congruent with their commitment patterns arising out of pre-Ervin times. Likewise, looking at the perceived importance of Watergate-type corruption as a major national political problem, we find a similar pattern. Our hypothesis was that the commitment measure would structure the priority placed upon this matter, with Nixon supporters placing greater emphasis on other types of issues. Table 5.9 shows that the expected pattern prevails.

Interestingly, the main difference between Table 5.9 and the thermometer data on Watergate personalities is the peculiar bifurcation between Democrats and non-Democrats. The normal progression found in Table 5.8 and expected in Table 5.9 as well does not materialize. The impact of voting for Nixon in 1972 washes out in the face of the stronger pull of party identification. Nixon Democrats and McGovern Democrats are nearly identical in their concern over Watergate. This seems to illustrate the power of long-range partisan commitment as a component of attitude formation and also shows the ephemeral nature of Democratic support received by Nixon in 1972.

TABLE 5.9
Concern about Watergate, by commitment level

Commitment Type	N	Percentage Mentioning Corruption as Number One or Two National Problem
McGovern Democrats	95	54%
Nixon Democrats	76	53%
Nixon Independents	43	30%
Nixon Republicans	109	30%

χ^2 significance = .0006

TABLE 5.10
Commitment type by belief news is biased

Commitment Type	N	Truthful	Biased
McGovern Democrats	84	55%	45%
Nixon Democrats	67	46%	54%
Nixon Independents	39	46%	54%
Nixon Republicans	100	37%	63%

χ^2 significance = .25

Belief That the News is Biased

A major means of reducing dissonance is to discredit the dissonating information by implying that it is inaccurate or in some way biased.[17] Our expectation was that those with higher levels of commitment to the administration would be more likely to feel that the national news media were biased and unfair in their reporting. Table 5.10 gives support to that hypothesis.

Looking at the relationship between belief in the veracity of news and attitude toward certain Watergate personalities, further positive patterns emerged. Table 5.11, for example, shows quite decisively that persons with positive feelings toward Senator Ervin were more likely to trust the news media. By the same token, those who disliked him also distrusted the news media. Our initial suspicion was that this pattern was the result of partisanship, that the supporters of Ervin were largely Democrats and his detractors largely Republicans. Controlling for commitment, however, produced no fundamental change in the relationship. As Table 5.12 shows, those who believed the news to be truthful were more likely to hold positive feelings towards Senator Ervin, regardless of voter or partisan type. It thus seems that dissonance was not the only cause of attitudes towards Senator Ervin, but that political trust was also a factor. Ervin's image as a man of integrity

123

TABLE 5.11
Feelings toward Ervin by belief in veracity of news

	Believe News Is Truthful	Believe News Is Biased
Positive Feelings toward Senator Ervin	58%	45%
Negative Feelings toward Senator Ervin	15%	29%

χ^2 significance = 0.009

TABLE 5.12
Positive feelings toward Ervin, by commitment type and belief in veracity of news reporting

	Believe News Truthful		Believe News Biased		Percentage Difference Across
	N	Percent Positive*	N	Percent Postive*	
McGovern Democrats	44	77%	36	56%	21%
Nixon Democrats	30	62%	35	55%	7%
Nixon Independents	18	44%	19	39%	5%
Nixon Republicans	36	36%	63	24%	12%

*Positive feelings are thermometer ratings of above 50.
χ^2 significance = .0001

affected some persons who would have been predisposed to think ill of him because of his role in exposing alleged administration corruption. While the commitment measure is critical in structuring attitudes toward Ervin, trust in him as an honest man also seems to have gained him some support.

Effects of Political Information

In a political dispute one often takes comfort in the belief that one's opponents are uninformed. Our data on Watergate attitudes offer no support for this hypothesis. Informed citizens—people who scored high on a test of political information—held the same opinions on President Nixon as the less informed, and among those with a positive or negative feeling, the informed citizens did not differ from the misinformed.

Rather than leave the analysis at this, however, we decided to see how the commitment measure affected the relationship between information and evaluation. When we controlled this, a definite and fascinating pattern emerged (see figure 5.3). Among those low on the

124

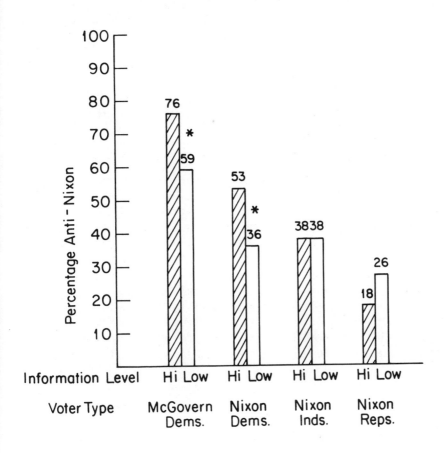

Figure 5.3 Unfavorable Feelings Toward Nixon

* Significant at .05 Level

dissonance measure (McGovern Democrats), the informed were more hostile to Nixon. Among those high on the dissonance measure (Nixon Republicans) the informed were less hostile to Nixon. At commitment level three (the independent Nixon voters) the well-informed and ill-informed had identical opinions.

Generally speaking, at the commitment extremes there is a tendency for well-informed respondents to intensify their commitment, or, at

TABLE 5.13
Feelings toward Nixon by level of information

	Misinformed	Informed*
Positive feelings toward President Nixon	35%	36%
Negative feelings toward President Nixon	47%	50%
Neutral feelings toward President Nixon	18%	14%

*The appendix shows the eight information items used in 1974. Four or more correct were scored as "informed."
χ^2 not significant at .05 level

least in the case of Nixon Republicans, to be less likely to abandon it. This is not surprising in the case of high dissonance groups who were presumably deluged with anti-administration revelations and news reports. We have already shown, however, the tendency for high dissonance groups to question the credibility of the news media. It is also possible that high dissonance groups engaged in selective reading, and sought out partisan news sources which fulfilled their need to know, while at the same time reducing their dissonance. Meanwhile, the low dissonance groups were doing the same by tuning in investigative reporters who uncovered Watergate wrongdoing.

In any case, both the high dissonance and low dissonance groups supported the classic finding that the more politically involved and informed elements of society have more coherent, or consistent belief systems.[18]

At the height of the Watergate crisis, humorist Art Buchwald wrote a column in which Richard Nixon ran hysterically throughout the White House berating his hapless aides because of their inability to locate his missing "mandate", which had been in the Oval Office just a short time before. In a sense, Buchwald's humor was not far off the mark, but in another sense it misreads the election of 1972. What Richard Nixon received in that year from Democrats and Independents was, in retrospect, not their pledges of support but merely their votes. A change in party identification is not a thing to be taken lightly. It often requires more than one election to firm up the conversion. Any Nixon Democrats who had harbored thoughts of a terminal break with their party and a reaffiliation with the Republicans quickly reconsidered in light of post-election developments. As we will show in a later section, the process of re-affirmation was reinforced by the decline of the economy and the subsequent re-emergence of the New Deal dimension.

The 1976 Presidential Primaries

Data collection for the 1976 presidential election was carried out in two steps—a major survey of attitudes in March, 1976, during the primary season, and a brief check back in November, 1976, to record the vote and ask a few questions about the campaign, the candidates, and the issues. We begin our analysis of that election with the presentation of attitudes during primary season. The analysis will build towards an explanation of the vote in the November election.

Candidates and Issues

Our primary season analysis began in the weeks immediately after the New Hampshire primary, which Carter and Ford won on February 24, 1976. During the period, the voters of Dearborn were not yet facing the need to choose a candidate, because the primary in Michigan was not scheduled until May. The respondents nonetheless had already gathered information and opinions on the candidates. In response to open ended information questions, two-thirds knew New Hampshire was the first primary, two-thirds knew Carter had carried the first Democratic primary, and 85% knew that Ford had won the first Republican primary. While Carter was not yet well known, 55% did know that his home state was Georgia.

The major concerns of the voters were economic, and this bode well for the Democrats in an election year. Fifty-four percent of our respondents thought unemployment, recession, inflation, or general economic concerns were the major problem facing the nation. Unemployment or recession was, in these spring months, cited twice as frequently as inflation. By November, as the local and national economies continued to improve, inflation would be perceived as a more serious problem than unemployment by a margin of three to two.[19]

The candidate thermometer scores in the primary season (Table 5.14) were most promising for Ford, Carter, Humphrey, and Percy (the latter two non-candidates). They were as chilling as New Hampshire snows for Wallace, Reagan, and Kennedy. Morris Udall was in the modest range but this was perhaps a result of the fact that so few

127

TABLE 5.14
Pre-primary thermometer scores (°)

Candidate	All Respondents	Strong Democrats	Weak Democrats	Non-Identifiers	Weak Republicans	Strong Republicans	Change from 1975s
Ford	57.2	48.5	54.6	62.3	63.6	71.9	−1
Humphrey	56.0	67.4	57.9	49.7	46.4	44.4	*
Percy	54.4	55.9	53.1	50.0	51.4	57.1	−3
Carter	53.4	58.9	51.2	54.6	50.4	47.7	+4
Jackson	52.8	58.9	50.0	51.4	48.2	50.2	−3
Udall	52.3	59.5	51.5	46.6	43.4	49.1	−1
Kennedy	49.9	64.4	48.2	41.0	38.3	34.0	−2
Reagan	49.2	44.5	43.3	55.0	55.8	56.6	−7
Wallace	46.9	47.2	48.9	54.9	42.1	46.0	−10
	N=169	N=46	N=37	N=52	N=87	

*Not asked in 1975

people were familiar with him. During five weeks of interviewing, Udall's thermometer scores rose until he matched and even passed Carter, a fact which presaged his close primary victory in Dearborn (though not in the metropolitan area).

A critical issue to keep in mind when evaluating thermometer scores is not merely the degree of support but the partisan location of that support. Two candidates with thermometer scores of 55°, for example, are of extremely different potential viability if one is strong across the political spectrum and the other is strong among his partisans but weak among the opposition and independent blocs.

Compare Charles Percy, for example, with Ronald Reagan. Percy was strong in all groups, ranging from 56° among strong Democrats to 57° among strong Republicans. Reagan, in contrast, was strong among Republicans and independents but was very unpopular among Democrats. Of course every candidate would like to enjoy popularity among independents and opposition members, but to a Republican such support is essential. A Republican who carries the Republican vote, splits the independents, and loses the Democrats will be defeated.

On the other side of the spectrum, the Democrats, favored by an almost two to one numerical advantage over their opposition are in a position to play a partisan game with some chance of winning. Hubert Humphrey and Edward Kennedy fall into this pattern. Both were viable or even intimidating opponents at one time, although they enjoy a support pattern which in a mirror image for a Republican would be deadly, since they showed little ability to penetrate opposition ranks.

In another useful measure of candidate popularity, respondents,

TABLE 5.15
Response to presidential candidates (%)

	First Choice	Most Rejected	Most Appealing as a Person	Least Appealing as a Person
Carter	9	1	16	4
Ford	27	9	16	5
Humphrey	13	6	9	12
Jackson	5	2	2	4
Kennedy	14	18	13	6
Reagan	8	8	17	6
Udall	3	1	3	1
Wallace	6	27	2	26

when asked which candidate they would *most* and *least* like to see elected president, turned to Ford twice as often as anyone else in the first instance, and against Wallace and Kennedy in the second (see Table 5.15).

Carter, fresh from his early primary victories, had the best ratio of support to rejection—nine to one. Similarly when asked which candidate was most appealing and pleasant *as a person,* and which was most unappealing and unpleasant, respondents were most attracted by Reagan, Carter, and Ford, and most repelled by George Wallace.

There was something pathetic about the 26% of the study who saw Wallace as an unappealing character. Wallace had carried Dearborn in the 1972 primary and had shocked the nation with his strong support in the Detroit suburbs, long a stronghold of such labor stalwarts as Humphrey and Kennedy. Now, a mere four years later, he was struggling for credibility in a populace which had clearly abandoned him. The Wallace era was over. The Carter era was on its way.

But as these data show, the Carter era had not yet arrived. At the time of this study, there were three voters holding out for Kennedy or Humphrey for every one voter who had joined the Carter bandwagon. The press spent a great deal of ink speculating on where the right-wing Wallace vote would go. It would have been far more profitable for them to speculate on where the left wing Kennedy-Humphrey vote would go.

It was also not certain what the status of Gerald Ford was. Though Reagan was not a viable threat in Dearborn, Ford's chances of election in the fall were not good. While his popularity was high among Republicans and independents, it dropped considerably among Democrats. Furthermore, when asked point blank if they were planning to vote for or against Ford, 55% of all respondents said against. While the strongest Republican, Ford's election looked in doubt even before the rise of Carter.

The electoral problems of this remarkably likeable native son illustrate the relative importance of long term and short term elements in presidential elections. Ford had a high level of personal credibility and a great deal of personal affection from the electorate. In contrast to his publicly removed predecessor, he was seen as a Gene Autry-type clean fighter who could win or lose on his merits and not by some secret conspiracy or dirty tricks.

But Gerald Ford's problem was that his obvious personal qualities were handicapped by the long range issues emerging in the country. In particular he was hurt by serious economic problems, especially in the cities, and the historic association of his party with a non-activist response to such problems. Given a perception in the public mind that serious problems such as these require government action, the public would be more likely to choose a candidate on the basis of hoped-for-action than personal charm. This would be especially true if the opposition candidate were equally trustworthy and attractive, a fact of which Jimmy Carter took full advantage.

Candidate Qualities

Most election studies over the past two decades have attempted to make some assessment of how the candidates as individuals have influenced electoral outcomes. The feeling thermometer in particular has contributed to a more precise measurement of this dimension. We believe, however, that even the feeling thermometer failed to capture the richness of the dimension as an explanatory variable. Perception of the candidate as a person, not just as a candidate, was not fully explored.

To study this more fully, we decided to use a modified version of the semantic differential.[20] In this technique, respondents are given pairs of opposite words and asked to place the candidate on a continuum somewhere between the two polar opposites. We used five of these opposite pairs, focusing on leadership and character qualities: How experienced did the candidates seem? How strong did each seem as a person? Was their leadership inspiring or dull? Did their ideas seem sensible, or risky and dangerous? Did they provide a good moral example for young people? In each of these five instances, respondents were asked to rate each candidate in one of four categories, such as, very experi-

TABLE 5.16
Leadership qualities of candidates (%)*

	Experienced	Strong	Inspiring Leader	Sensible Ideas	Good Moral Example
Ford	85	74	42	77	85
Reagan	58	74	64	52	83
Kennedy	75	64	70	62	50
Humphrey	87	66	53	71	86
Carter	46	66	62	66	86
Wallace	61	64	60	30	56

*Reported here are the combined percentage score of the favorable categories, for example, very experienced and experienced.

enced, experienced, inexperienced, or very inexperienced. In Table 5.16 we see the percentage in the positive (i.e., top two) categories.

As we have mentioned already, candidate evaluation is one of the key components of voter decisions, along with issues and party. It is especially important at the presidential level where voters believe high stakes are at risk. The president is not comparable to a congressman or mayor, in whom we may tolerate moral corruption, personal weakness, or mediocrity. The president is not only the symbol of the nation's values, but also the person whose finger is on the trigger. Untested mettle, a tendency to rashness, moral laxity, or a suspected tendency to break under pressure can all disqualify an otherwise well-qualified candidate. Gerald Ford, who seemed to put people to sleep, was otherwise seen as an eminently qualified candidate. Ronald Reagan, experienced, strong and inspiring, raised serious doubts in almost half the populace that he might be a "risky" chief executive. Carter had much going for him—he was strong, inspiring, sensible, moral. He was lacking only in experience, an image deficit which could be overcome as the pros of the party rallied behind him with endorsements and praise, or through the addition of a "heavyweight" running mate such as Mondale.

In trying to assess the image qualities of the candidates, one has to take into account the relative impact of images. A good image—even one irrelevant to the immediate demands of office—can help a candidate. For example, being seen as friendly can be an asset even if friendliness is not required in the post. On the other hand, there are certain innate qualities required of a person to effectively perform the tasks of the office. Good judgement is essential in one to be trusted with so much power. Finally, there are ways in which a candidate can

131

be *relatively* hurt or helped by an image—even a position-irrelevant one—which is different from that of the opponent. Thus a close election between two otherwise identical candidates might hinge on a superficial quality such as physical appearance.

Therefore, as in so many other things, we have to look at those things which help, those things which hurt, and those things which neither hurt nor help but which, in the absence of other considerations, are desirable. The only candidates who had serious image problems were Reagan and Wallace, and perhaps Kennedy. Reagan and Wallace were handicapped by their image as potentially "risky" decision makers. Kennedy's obvious weakness in the "moral example" category is not inherently disqualifying since it is not office-connected, but it constituted a major weakness in his overall electability and surely played a role in his decision not to be a candidate.

The weaknesses of Ford, Carter, and Humphrey, in contrast, were minor and could easily be overcome as the campaign progressed. Any of these three would have been strong candidates with few image problems. Reagan and Kennedy would also have been strong candidates with overall images which provided definite pluses to their campaign.

Issue-Position Images

Turning from candidate character to candidate position on issues (see Table 5.17), we see three issue dimensions based on the seven-point scales discussed earlier. The dimensions include busing, a national health care program, and general liberalism-conservatism. Health care is conceived as a classic New Deal issue which was likely to be a point of contention between parties and candidates in 1976. Busing was a cross-cutting cleavage from the period of party disruption, 1968–1972, whose importance in 1976 was worth examining. Liberalism was a composite measure which seems to tap a general ideological orientation.

In the table we show the location of the average voter, the average supporter of a candidate, and the perceived position of the parties and the candidates.*

*The table had several flaws. It omitted Republican challengers (Reagan) entirely and studied only the *supporters* of Democratic aspirants, while asking *all* respondents where Gerald Ford (the assumed candidate of the Republican party) stood. These flaws were anticipated in advance but could not be overcome without seriously lengthening the questionnaire. It also seemed that in the early stages of the primary race, when the country was considering a host of often unknown candidates, a question such as "Where does Birch Bayh stand on this issue?" would often be met with a blank stare, even though Bayh was considered a serious and viable candidate by many observers.

Issue positions during 1972 primary

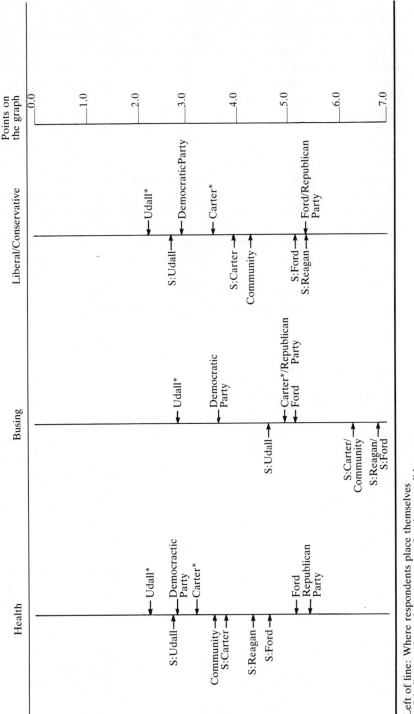

Left of line: Where respondents place themselves
  S indicates where the supporters of a given candidate are.
Right of Line: Perceived positions of candidates and parties
  *indicates where supporters of these candidates see them.
  Other positions are where the total sample places them, not just supporters.
Slash (/) indicates that two candidates: parties are at the same point on the scale.

The table shows the typical voter on the conservative side on busing at 6.3, in the middle on liberalism at 4.2, and liberal on health care at 3.6. Comparing voter location with perceived candidate and party positions, respondents were closer to Ford and the Republicans on busing, and closer to the Democrats on health care. The perceived positions of Carter and Ford were both excellent for winning voter support. On health care, Carter's perceived position was closer to the typical voter than Ford, with Carter slightly on the liberal side, Ford slightly on the conservative. Udall was perceived as being more liberal than Carter, as was the Democratic party. On busing, all candidates were seen as more liberal than the community, with Ford slightly closer to the community than Carter. Udall and the Democratic Party are seen as way out of line. On the overall liberalism, Carter and Ford and the two parties are equidistant from the community, with Udall well on the liberal side.

Thus, on the issues, Udall was perceived as being somewhat distant, while Carter and Ford were close to mainstream community thinking. It is interesting to note that Udall, in spite of being off center, raced Carter to the finish line in several primaries, including the one in Dearborn, which he carried. Reagan, who in contrast was very close to Ford on location, also managed a photo finish.

The 1976 Primaries: The Vote

By the time Dearborn's primary was held, the races had been narrowed down considerably. Ford and Reagan were locked in a fierce two-way battle for the Republican nomination; Udall and Carter were the sole combatants on the Democratic side. The Republicans had a choice of two conservatives; the Democrats, of a liberal and a moderate. Since Michigan had an open primary (a person could vote in either party's primary without being a registered party member), it was possible for party members to switch over and engage in 'raiding,' i.e., voting in the other party's primary. This had happened in 1972 when over 200,000 non-Democrats voted in the Democratic primary and gave the state's primary nod to Wallace, in spite of extensive hostility to Wallace within the party leadership. But 1976 was different, since in 1972 there had been only one meaningful presidential primary race. In 1976 there were two, both creating a great deal of excitement. Given this situation, we could expect Democrats and Republicans to stay fairly close to their home camps, with very few crossovers.

The real focus of our data analysis then is twofold: First, what divi-

sions would emerge within the parties? Would Udall and Carter supporters split along liberal/conservative lines or would they divide on
the basis of personality and leadership characteristics? If the latter
were the case, then we should find few, if any, differences on issues
between the two sets of supporters. And what about the Reagan/Ford
division within the Republican party? The media were suggesting that
Reagan, a darling of the Right, was much more conservative than
Ford, who was philosophically conservative but whose positions were
moderated by the responsibilities of presidential office. Again, one
could look for either an ideological division within the party, or for a
division on the basis of personal qualities, leadership and 'winability.'

Second, what divisions occur between the parties? Of particular concern would be the extent of unity or division on "old" issues such as
the role of the government in the economy or providing social welfare
programs versus "new" issues such as morality, racial conflict, crime,
the role of women. Again, to review, if the new issues were neutralized or unimportant in the two races, we would expect that in the
general election the natural Democratic majority would be triumphant
on the basis of economic and social welfare issues. If on the other
hand, people were worried about crime and race, were satisfied with
the performance of the economy under the Ford administration, and
felt that Ford's performance in maintaining the peace was satisfactory,
then the Democratic party could split and the advantage could go to
the Republicans.

Before we examine these divisions, however, let us turn briefly to
the public image of the parties. Again, remember that not all voters
respond to issues. A large component of the voting public is devoid of
issue orientation. These voters respond instead to general issue images
or to perceived performance capabilities. Such perceptions can be critical in determining the outcome of an election.

The Power of Party

Suppose a political scientist was given a group of 1000 voters and
allowed to interview them extensively over a period of time. Suppose
also that the political scientist is able to find out anything needed to
help predict how these people will vote in an upcoming election—their
income, their education, their jobs, their position on the issues, their
religion, their memberships. When it was all over, the political scientist
would discover that in most elections the *best single predictor* of how
an individual will vote is that individual's political party identification.[21]

135

TABLE 5.18
Perception of the parties (%)

Are the parties different?	
Yes	73
Which is the party of peace?	
Democrats	17
Republicans	25
No difference	59
Which is the party of prosperity?	
Democrats	48
Republicans	22
No difference	30
Which is the party of people such as yourself?	
Democrats	42
Republicans	16
No difference	42
Which is the party to control waste in government?	
Democrats	13
Republicans	27
No difference	61

It is thus of critical importance—as we have said before—to find out the extent to which the party loyalty factor is holding strong. In the past few presidential elections, party has been a weakened component of voting behavior. In 1952 and 1956 Dwight Eisenhower induced millions of Democrats to vote the Republican ticket; in 1964, Barry Goldwater drove millions of Republicans out of the party, as George McGovern did for the Democrats in 1972; in 1968, George Wallace ran on a third party ticket and split the Democratic electorate. To columnist David Broder (and to others) it seemed that "the party's over."[22]

But 1976 seems to have re-established the party as an element in voter decisions. The Watergate scandal had been a humiliating experience, not only for Republicans, but for those millions of Democrats who had voted for Richard Nixon and lived to regret it. The economic recession of 1974 and 1975, which had not entirely abated by 1976, was still fresh in the people's minds. Many observers were saying that 1976 would be the first election since 1960 in which Democrats would vote the Democratic ticket and Republicans would vote the Republican ticket. Table 5.18 shows how voters perceived the parties in March and April of 1976. As we can see, the advantage, such as it was, was running in the direction of the Democrats.

The powerful issues which had helped the Republican's ticket so much in 1972—peace and prosperity—were now no longer in their column. The peace issue had been neutralized so that a majority of people felt both parties were equally able in this area, and the economic issue was clearly running in a Democratic direction. Almost three-fourths of the people saw the parties as being fundamentally different, a fact which must inevitably hurt the Republicans; over 60% saw no difference in the ability of the parties to control wasteful government expenditure—a key Ford position which Carter had also made a basic issue. On a final question—which party can best help people such as yourself—a scant 16% chose the Republicans.

Perception of the Parties

Although party identification is one of the most important long range factors in determining vote, voters are subject to short term factors which can produce deviations in party loyalty. Table 5.19 presents the results of the 1976 primary as compared with party image.* From this table it is easy to see that Republican voters were suffering from a serious crisis of confidence, just at a time when Democratic voters were convinced their party knew what to do. Look, for example, at the following pattern: when asked whether they preferred a good Democrat or a good Republican in 1976, 83% of the Democrats stuck with their party, but only 68% of the Republicans did. This is an unusual pattern, since historically Republicans have been more party-oriented than Democrats. It reflected the crisis which was upon the Republicans as a result of Watergate, the Nixon recession, and the conflict between Ford and Reagan. It was a serious omen.

On the major areas of party image, the Republicans were also in serious shape. Eighty-seven percent of the Democrats thought there was a real difference between the parties. As mentioned earlier, it is critical to Republican fortunes to woo away a sizeable bloc of Democrats if there is to be any chance of winning the presidency. This can be done only by persuading the public either that there is no difference between the parties or that the Republicans are stronger on key issues

---

*In looking at this and subsequent tables, the reader should use a certain amount of caution. Voting preferences are based upon recall, as recorded in early November, 1976, a full six months after the primary vote. Recall data of this type is often quite "soft" in the sense that people frequently forget for whom they voted. In a presidential race this is not nearly as serious because the race is more important and the voter more likely to remember correctly. There is also a practical problem: fewer people vote in a primary, leaving a smaller number in any given table. The χ^2 significance level will assist the reader in deciding how much trust to put in a given pattern.

TABLE 5.19
Party image among primary voters

Item	Voted in which Primary?			Voters in Democratic primary who supported			Voters in Republican primary who supported		
	D	R	χ^2 Sig	Carter	Udall	χ^2 Sig	Ford	Reagan	χ^2 Sig
This fall, would you prefer to vote for a good D (left %) or a good R (right %)?	83/17	11/68	.00	83/13	85/9	.43	16/74	22/48	.01
Are the parties different? (% "yes")	87	65	.003	87	94	.06	63	63	.62
Which is the party of prosperity?*	73/6/21	25/48/27	.0000	74/6/20	73/6/21	.79	19/54/27	42/21/37	.01
Which is the party of the common people?*	68/6/26	11/36/53	.0000	68/6/26	50/9/41	.85	10/35/55	17/33/50	.08
Which is the best party to control waste and inefficiency in government?*	24/15/61	2/47/51	.0000	35/15/50	9/18/73	.04	3/45/52	0/50/50	.79
Which is the party of peace?*	26/9/65	3/41/66	.0000	28/11/61	25/6/69	.71	1/45/54	8/29/63	.0000

*Left figure is percent preferring Democrats; middle is percent preferring Republicans; right is percent who see no difference.

such as peace or prosperity. On both of these points, the Republicans were vulnerable.

On the key issue of peace, on which Nixon scored so well in 1972, the Republicans failed to carry a majority of their own bloc. Republican and Democratic voters seemed to agree that both parties were equally qualified to maintain the peace, though the Republican party does do marginally better. On the other key issue of prosperity, Democrats were ahead in the race for support. Almost three-fourths of all Democratic voters supported their party's efforts in this area, but only a quarter of Republicans did the same for their party. Surprisingly, almost half of all Republican voters had more confidence in the Democratic party than in their own leaders.

On the other areas of party image, the results were mixed, but again, not particularly favorable to the Republicans. Regarding which is the party of the common people, Democrats did about twice as well as Republicans. Only on the issue of which party could best control waste in government do we see Republican strength, and even the Republicans give a vote of only 47% to their party.

Turning to divisions within the parties, the most interesting pattern which emerged was the appearance of a weak right wing within the Republican party. Reagan supporters were less supportive of their party (48% of Reaganites and 74% of Ford supporters preferred a Republican victory in 1976), and Reaganites had less enthusiasm for the party's abilities in the field of peace and prosperity, two key issues on which Ford was basing his campaign.

On the other side, the Democrats were less divided. Carter and Udall supporters both were inclined to support a Democrat for the presidency, both saw big differences between the parties, and both felt the Democrats were the party of prosperity. On the issue of peace, they saw no difference between the parties, a significant improvement over 1972 when party regulars lost faith in the ability of party leaders to end the war. On supporting the common people, there was some doubt among the Udall voters, but not enough to cause them to trust the Republicans. Carter people, on the other hand, doubted that the Democrats could control government inefficiency, a key Carter plank.

Overall, we see a Republican party that was wracked with doubts and insecurities, and a Democratic party united around a conviction that it could do a good job. In neither case does there appear to be significant "within" divisions, though the Reagan voters betrayed a lack of trust in the incumbent's performance in office.

139

Economic and Social Welfare Issues

As mentioned in chapter one, the parties have been divided since the 1930's over two key issues: how much should the government intervene in the economy, and how much should the government do through specific programs to help people maintain a better life. In years when these issues are primary in voter thinking, the Democrats have usually done well. The experience of recent years indicated, however, that there might be a conservative wing developing within the Democratic party. Carter had spoken against waste and mismanagement and had sometimes presented the image of a fiscal and social welfare conservative. Udall, on the other hand, had emerged as an articulate spokesman for the liberal position within the party, urging that the government intervene to correct inequities in distribution and to prevent abuse by private economic groups.

The results as shown in Table 5.20 are striking. On no single issue did the Reagan-Ford voters disagree at a statistically significant level; on no single issue did the Carter-Udall voters disagree at a statistically significant level; but on every single issue except one there was a statistically significant level of disagreement between Democrats and Republicans. Clearly, the impact of this dimension on the parties is great. Suggestions that Carter and Udall were pulling from different wings of the party on these issues seem exaggerated; suggestions that a conservative Reagan and a moderate Ford were attracting different voters seems incorrect.

It is hard to make observations about this table which are not obvious. One point worth making, however, relates to the link between what we see here and the chance of a party realignment. A realignment would occur, according to Sundquist, when old issues fade and new issues emerge. As we can see, the old issues remain powerful and are still capable of activating sentiments and identities which originated almost 50 years ago. Realignments do not have to happen on schedule or at all. The natural evolutions and changes which occur in societies make such realignments likely but not obligatory. If the problems of society remain essentially the same, the party system can be periodically reinforced by crises which emphasize, rather than undermine, the fundamental cleavage which created the party system in the first place. What seems to have happened between 1972 and 1976 was the reinforcement of party identifications, the re-emergence of the old cleavage, and the relative decline in salience of the new cleavages of 1972.

TABLE 5.20

1976 primary vote, by position on economic issues (%)

Item	Voted in which primary?			Voters in Democratic party who supported . . .			Voters in Republican party who supported . . .		
	D	R	χ^2 Sig Level	Carter	Udall	χ^2 Sig Level	Ford	Reagan	χ^2 Sig Level
Government not as efficient as private business	79	94	.01	85	71	.46	95	96	.95
Government provide health care	86	75	.05	83	88	.59	72	83	.48
Government provide jobs	76	42	.00	71	82	.58	45	38	.41
Government guaranteed income	62	36	.002	62	62	.96	39	29	.29
Government provide housing loans	67	37	.0003	67	69	.18	37	42	.66
Government provide educational loans	71	65	.38	74	71	.74	65	64	.75
Government job scale (positions 1–3)	45	15	.006	41	55	.61	13	18	.55
Government medical care scale (positions 1–3)	64	40	.0003	68	67	.09	27	38	.91
Government quit programs	55	77	.007	64	41	.24	75	83	.15

The 1976 Vote

In an earlier section we showed that Watergate attitudes were primarily a function of the behavior and identification structure associated with the 1972 election time period. Commitments at the time were closely associated with how one reacted to accusations of wrongdoing in the White House at a later time. In a like manner, we would suggest that a most useful structure of analysis is to view the 1976 election within the framework of 1972, with particular emphasis on those voters who supported one party's candidate in 1972 but another party's candidate in 1976.

Of critical importance, of course, are the Nixon-Carter switch voters, who, if our expectations are correct, should share many characteristics with the Nixon Democrats of 1972. We would expect most of them to be Democrats; we would also expect them to be somewhat more conservative than regular two-time Democratic voters on "new issues" such as crime, race, and life style. On such issues we would expect Nixon-Carter voters to be conservative in the manner of the Nixon-Ford voters. On the New Deal dimension, however, we would expect the same Nixon-Carter voters to be liberal like the McGovern-Carter group.

McGovern-Ford switch voters are hard to categorize. We can think of no major ideological or issue motive which would cause such a pattern. Our expectation is that such voters would be motivated by loyalty to the presidency, by a high opinion of Gerald Ford's honesty and integrity, or by some similar orientation to the personalities of the candidates. Unfortunately, their numbers are so few in our panel that we were unable to test any of these hypotheses and have omitted them from our analysis.

Two-time Democratic voters or two-time Republican voters, in contrast, should fall into clearcut partisan or left and right configurations. These are the hard core. The Democrats stuck with McGovern in the face of enormous pressure to defect, and the Republicans stuck with Ford in spite of an attractive Democratic nominee. These are not the types of people who shift at a whim, or who abandon ship because of temporary setbacks. They are most likely committed liberals and committed conservatives, who vote issues more than personalities, and who are not easily seduced away by short-term fluctuations in party or candidate popularity. In actually looking at those who voted for major party candidates and who also voted in both elections, we found the following pattern:

TABLE 5.21
*Presidential vote in 1972 and 1976**

		1972 vote		
		Nixon	McGovern	
Vote in 1976	Ford	51.0%	5.6%	201
	Carter	15.8%	27.6%	154
		237	118	n=355

*In looking at data which report patterns across time the reader should focus on the relationships within the table and should not assume that the relative number of Ford and Carter supporters reflects the pattern in the whole community (in fact, Ford carried the community of Dearborn by a narrow margin, not the landslide that appears in Table 5.21). A panel study such as this inevitably has a "mortality" built into it, meaning that a certain proportion of respondents contacted once are never contacted again. In general, the types of people lost are those of the lower socio-economic classes. This means in simple terms that as our study progressed across the years the sample became more Republican in identification.

This problem is not important in a table in which we compare, for example, vote with issue. Then the results are in correlations so that the base percentages are not relevant. In a table such as 5.21, however, the reporting of a biased base could be misleading. As discussed in chapter four, the control group used in 1975 allowed us to measure for bias in our correlations, and we found that panel mortality did not distort correlations.

The critical element, about which there had been so much speculation, is clearly there—the Nixon-to-Carter switch. A quick breakdown of Jimmy Carter's vote showed what happened: 24% of all Nixon voters cast their ballots for Carter in 1976; of all Carter voters, a full 36% had been Nixon voters previously. Although these results are for the Dearborn panel and do not replicate national trends, what they show in general is essentially what happened elsewhere: Carter was able to woo back enough Nixon voters to squeak by with a narrow victory.

What we would like to do now is what we have already suggested— look closely at these voters to see who they were in terms of issues and orientations. It is in this area that we should gain some insight into the nature of the Carter victory as well as the condition of the party coalitions.

Issues and the Vote Shift

It is clear from our analysis that the 1976 election re-established the political importance of New Deal-type issues, and enabled Jimmy

143

TABLE 5.22
*1972/1976 voter type compared with position on federal activism
(% liberal)* *

Item	Voter Type		
	Nixon-Ford	Nixon-Carter	McGovern-Carter
New Deal Index (high)	38	66	77
Support more regulation of industry	17	38	46
Favor federal control of oil companies	14	34	49

*All statistically significant at .05 level or better

Carter to re-integrate Nixon-voting liberals into the Democratic camp. Table 5.22 illustrates what happened. In this table we see the five-item New Deal index and two one-to-seven self-placement issue scales.

The pattern seen here is very similar to that seen in the 1972 election typology reported earlier in this chapter. Specifically, we note that the whole political spectrum, with the exception of the hard core Republican vote bloc, are on the liberal side of the federal activism scale. A quick comparison of McGovern-Carter voters and Nixon-Carter voters show the essential similarity of viewpoint of these two groups.

Even on such a controversial topic as federal control of the oil industry, where most respondents react negatively, we find that the ratio of straight Democratic voters in favor compared with straight Republican voters in favor is 4.5 to 1.0. Furthermore, the distance between one group mean and another illustrates the extent of disagreement over these basic issues. Comparing Nixon-Carter voters with straight Democratic voters and with straight Republican voters, we find them in each case significantly closer to the Democrats than to their Republican counterparts. On the New Deal index, for example, they are 28 points from the Nixon-Ford voters, but only 11 points from the McGovern-Carter bloc.

As we have seen earlier, this same attitude pattern prevailed in 1972 but at the time these social welfare issues were not powerful enough to bind liberals together behind the McGovern candidacy. By 1976, however, these forces were much stronger and produced a very consistent and predictable pattern of voting.

On law and order and racial issues, the Nixon-Carter swing voters were much more like Republican regulars. This explains the support

TABLE 5.23
New issues and the vote (% conservative)

Item	Nixon-Ford	Nixon-Carter	McGovern-Carter	x^2 Significance
Police search (support)	69	64	49	.02
Judges too soft (agree)	92	97	79	.01
Capital punishment (favor)	79	77	53	.01
Inter-racial marriage (morally wrong)	22	27	6	.01
Busing (strongly opposed)	70	76	50	.06
X-rated movies (opposed)	78	78	62	.13
Abortion (opposed)	26	25	32	.65
Marijuana users (low)	41	32	32	.70
Women's lib (low)	39	38	15	.02
Sex education (opposed)	27	19	26	.16
Homosexuals (low)	23	27	22	.97
Women better in the home	39	68	44	.00
Gross Average	50.4	47.5	36.5	

the swing voters gave to Nixon and Agnew in the law and order year of 1972. Table 5.23 shows the patterns.

Nixon-Carter swing voters are actually more conservative than Nixon-Ford "regular Republicans" on almost half of the issues. The average separation between these two sets of voters across the whole range of issues is about 3%. In contrast, the gap between the switchers and the McGovern-Carter bloc is about eleven points, with the regular Democrats being more liberal on all but two of the issues.

These rather rough statistical comparisons are designed to illustrate a key fact of the 1976 election: Carter had clearly plastered over a huge cleavage in the ranks of his supporters by drawing in these Nixon-Carter voters. He did so by emphasizing the state of the nation's economy and by preventing social concerns from splitting his followers.

The Role of Materialism

We have argued that voters are being whipsawed by their intense concerns about two sets of issues: law and order, race and life styles on

145

the one hand, and economic disruption on the other. A concern about law and order would be classified in the previously discussed Inglehart framework as a safety need; a concern about economic problems would be classified as a security need. These are both "lower needs," in contrast to such concerns as love and self-actualization. We would expect that switch voters would be more motivated by lower, or materialistic, needs. This is indeed the case. While the major difference that emerges is the distinction between the post-materialism of McGovern voters and the more materialist needs of Nixon voters, a second pattern is that vote switchers emerge year after year as consistently more materialist than even Nixon-Ford regulars.

Thus, as we observed earlier, the Democratic party, always a coalition of diverse points of view, finds itself the home of both poles on this particular value dimension. If, as we suspect, the country is suffering a crisis of cultural values, induced by widespread social change and economic disruption, then this issue could re-emerge in the future. The fact that it did not correlate with the vote in 1976 attests to the impact of non-cultural issues in that election and also to the conservative personalities of both major party candidates. We would anticipate that the issue would re-emerge at some time in the future, perhaps as a demand for economic security or as a part of the ongoing property-tax revolt.

Predicting the Vote

Earlier we developed a multivariate model for the 1972 vote; we have done the same for the 1976 vote. The 1976 model is an elaboration of the earlier effort. This elaboration is made possible by the additional questions we were able to ask in 1976, specifically the semantic-differential items discussed earlier. Our expectation was that voter partisanship would cause higher ratings for the candidates of one's own party. In turn, these evaluations of character traits should affect the overall comparison of the two candidates, as measured in their thermometer scores. Finally, we included in the analysis perceived ability to manage the economy. We expected this to be an important cause of the vote in a year when the economy was a big issue.

We also expected that voter opinion on this would be influenced by how liberal the voter was on New Deal issues such as "should the government do all in its power to insure a job to those who want work?" After all, Carter and Ford were arguing about whether more

146

TABLE 5.24
Materialism by voter type

Materialism indicator	Nixon-Carter	Nixon-Ford	McGovern-Carter
Post-bourgeois, 1974	46%	36%	20%
Self-actualization, 1974	58%	56%	37%
Self-actualization, 1975	62%	53%	42%
Post-bourgeois, 1976	35%	31%	23%

All significant at the .05 level except self-actualization, 1974 which has a χ^2 significance of .11.

emphasis should be put on providing jobs or fighting inflation. Well-informed Americans were basing their votes on this issue. And this was a policy trade-off on which voter choice is regularly converted into government action.[23] It made sense that voters who were liberal on the New Deal dimension would favor Carter as the better manager for the economy, while conservatives on this dimension would favor Ford. It also made sense that Democrats would think of Carter as better for the economy, while Republicans would prefer Ford.

With the addition of these new items, we could take a fresh look at the classic question: is the most important predictor of the vote party identification, candidate qualities, or issue position?

We tested the model by using the same technique (path analysis) we had used for 1972. As can be seen in Figure 5.4, issues had no significant effect on the election. One issue dimension—New Deal—was correlated with the presidential vote, but its significance disappeared once we controlled for party identification. Whether Carter or Ford was seen to be better for the economy was indeed a major determinant of the vote. But voters' opinions on this question of economic management were caused by party identification, not by issue positions. Those who thought Ford was better were Republicans, not economic conservatives. For these reasons, we treat the opinion on whether Carter or Ford is better for the economy as a partisan campaign "theme," not an "issue" in the campaign. And, just as issues of government involvement in the economy had no significant effect on the election, cross-cutting social issues—busing, post-materialism, and women's liberation—had no effect either. In short, none of the issue clusters identified in chapter three nor any other issue in the questionnaire had a significant impact on the 1976 presidential election after controlling for other causal variables in the model. Instead, the election outcome was determined by partisanship, by evaluation of candidate character, and by campaign themes woven in the media and shaped by partisan forces.

Figure 5.4 Path Coefficients Showing Causes of 1979 Vote **

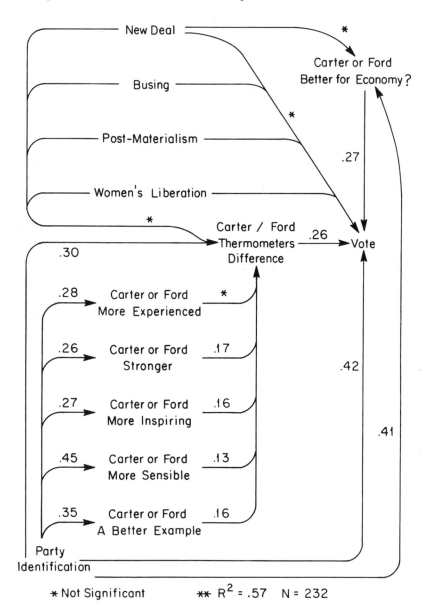

* Not Significant   ** R^2 = .57   N = 232

The most important of these determinants was party identification. Its direct impact (measured by the path coefficient of .42) is much stronger than any other direct cause of the vote. It also had strong indirect effects, since it helped to shape the other two causes of the vote, the overall thermometer comparison of the two candidates, and the judgment on which candidate would manage the economy better. Taking these direct and indirect effects together, as in Figure 5.5, we see that the total impact of party identification was more than twice as important as any other determinant of the vote.

Perception of candidate's character also had a significant impact on the vote. This impact was more important than the impact of the issues, but less important than the impact of party identification. The public seemed to be searching for a president who could play many roles: a strong national leader; a good moral example; an inspiring spokesman; and a sensible man who would not lead the nation down dangerous roads.[24] On the other hand, experience did not seem as crucial to the voters. This was lucky for Carter, because as we have seen, voters give him very low marks on experience. But America has long been a land of semi-professional politicians[25] and Carter was not significantly wounded by this liability. Strength, inspiration, moral example, and sensible thinking each had about equal influence on the overall evaluation of Carter and Ford, which in turn had a major impact on the voter's decision. Hence, while issues in the pure sense were not affecting the vote, we have evidence that the voters were doing a complex job of evaluating many dimensions of the personal qualities of the nominees.

In summary, three variables—party, who's best at the economy, and candidates' thermometer differences—are enough to correctly "predict" over 90% of the Ford vote and over 80% of the Carter vote. In other words, using the statistical technique of discriminant analysis, and providing the computer with each voter's position on these three variables, the computer can correctly predict, in over 90% of the cases, that someone who ultimately voted for Ford in November would in fact do so. For Carter voters, our predictive power drops off slightly, but we still get 80% of them right. This is especially impressive in that we designed this model a year before the November 1976 elections, and asked all but one of the questions over four months before either candidate was nominated for President.

But one of our predictions did not come true: issues had neither a direct nor an indirect impact on the vote. In a year when the economy was such an important issue, we expected that the New Deal issues

149

FIGURE 5.5
Direct and indirect effects on the 1976 vote

Predictors, In Order Of Importance	Effects		Intervening Variable	Combined Total
	Direct	Indirect		
Party identification	.42	.11	Carter or Ford better for the economy?	.61
		.08	Difference of Carter and Ford thermometers	
Carter or Ford better for economy?	.27			.27
Difference between Carter and Ford thermometers	.26			.26
Carter or Ford stronger as a person?		.04	Difference of Carter and Ford thermometers	.04
Carter or Ford a more inspiring leader?		.04	Difference of Carter and Ford thermometers	.04
Carter or Ford a better example for young people?		.04	Difference of Carter and Ford thermometers	.04
Carter or Ford more sensible?		.03	Difference of Carter and Ford thermometers	.03

which had given rise to the current alignment would affect the voting patterns that restored that alignment. We were wrong. Nor did the issues have an indirect effect. We had certainly expected that a liberal voter would think Carter better for the economy and a conservative voter would tend to think Ford better. This was not true. The crucial opinion on which candidate would be better for the economy was not affected by any of the voter's opinions on the issues. The major explanatory variable in this area was party identification, which accounted for 27% of all variance. The only other variable that seemed to influence this attitude was perception of news ("In the last few months, have you heard mostly good news or mostly bad news about the economy?"), which explained another 3%. This suggests that the news media, assisted by partisan preferences, have more effect on a voter's judgement about candidate economic capabilities than the voter's actual economic hardships, ideological position, social class, or union membership (all non-significant).[26] Perceived economic capability thus was not an ideological issue, but a free floating campaign theme, shaped by partisanship and by campaign advertising and image building.

The above model of the 1976 election was based on the classic contrast of partisanship, personality, and economic issues. It includes *a priori* expectations and explains much variance, but is not the best possible model. The best model is one we found by trial and error with the data. Let us shift, then, from the model we laid out deductively to the one found by the inductive process of trial and error.

The Inductive Model: The Impact of Image

As stated earlier, we can predict voters' choices in 1976 by moving away from perception of candidate character and New Deal type issues and toward candidate image and party identification.[27] This new model is presented in Figure 5.6. Despite its simplicity, it is more accurate than the earlier model. As before, party identification is given a prominant place as the dominant driving force of the model. It represents the existing disposition of the voter before the 1976 campaign begins. It directly influences the presidential vote. It also has indirect influence: it helps shape the thermometer ratings of the candidates and helps determine voter perception of which candidate is more honest, which candidate cares more "for the common people and their problems," and which candidate will be better at "keeping down the cost of government and holding down taxes." Those three perceptions of the candidates, along with party identification and thermometer ratings, do a very successful job of predicting the 1976 outcome. Knowing these five things, we can correctly predict 96% of the Carter vote and 91% of the Ford vote.[28] Adding who is better for the economy makes for a marginally better prediction. No other variables can improve that prediction.

In short, three questions—who is more honest, more caring, and better for taxes—seem to have had a profound effect on the election. We must be a bit more cautious in assessing their importance because we did find them inductively. In assessing them, we will consider how they came into our study, which candidate benefited from each of them, what causes voters' opinions on them, and how important each of them is in determining the presidential vote.

The three images of the candidates were part of a set of themes we

151

observed during the course of the 1976 campaign. In that campaign, we saw each side trying to convince the voters that its candidate was more caring, would handle the economy more competently, was more intelligent, was more honest, was better able to contain taxes, and would do more for peace. Each of these campaign themes was an attempt to create a favorable image for one candidate or a bad image for the other. These campaign themes could not be generated by the market research teams around each candidate until he and his opponent had been nominated. Only then would it be clear what the advantages and liabilities of each side were going to be. Once these campaign themes took shape in the fall of 1976, we were able to note them, and include them in our post-election survey of six questions on candidate images.

Once the images were a part of our study, we could examine which candidate benefited from each of them. Table 5.25 analyzes these images, or themes, of the campaign. Carter scored better, as a Democrat normally would, on caring for the common people. Ford scored better on keeping the peace, as one might expect, given his years of experience in the White House and on Capitol Hill, and Carter's lack of experience in foreign affairs. Neither candidate could gain a big advantage on the personal traits of being intelligent or making honest speeches and promises. Instead, while many intellectuals were belittling Ford's intelligence, a majority of voters perceived no difference between Ford and Carter on this quality. Ford did hold an edge on honesty, despite Carter's promise never to tell a lie to the American people, but here too the greatest number of people thought the two men equally honest. On the bread-and-butter issues, Ford held the edge on controlling taxes, Carter on keeping the economy healthy. Interestingly, Carter was stronger on the economy even though most people thought inflation was a more serious problem than unemployment, and Carter had a program to reduce unemployment that Ford claimed would speed up inflation.

While voter images of the candidates are themselves largely a product of party identification, these images also are partially independent of the influence of party. As seen in Figure 5.6, party identification has an especially strong impact on who is seen as more honest and who is seen as better for taxes. Who cares more for the common man is less influenced by partisanship, but still, one suspects, more shaped by partisanship than by any other factor. Quite likely news media reporting also plays a critical role, as was the case in the economic management question discussed earlier.

152

TABLE 5.25
% thinking Carter or Ford better

	Caring	Economy	Intelligence	Honesty	Taxes	Peace
Carter	55	46	18	17	31	10
Ford	20	36	21	39	45	61
Equal or don't know	25	18	61	45	23	29

In items of predicting the vote, the question on keeping down taxes is the strongest direct predictor of any variable we collected in 3½ years of study. This simple truth may show that the 1978 tax revolt was already well underway in 1976. Jimmy Carter was elected on a platform of government efficiency and a balanced budget. These pledges may have had more importance than has been realized. President Ford, as a Republican, also won votes on his pledges to keep down the cost and size of government. The dominance of the tax limitation theme in our causal analysis suggests that the media were wrong in thinking that the tax revolt of 1978 originated in California with "Proposition 13 fever." It is fashionable to see California as the future of the United States and to point out that many cultural innovations originate there. It is also true that California was the first of many states to hold a referendum that limited taxes and that the California revolt went further than the revolts in the states that followed its lead. Nevertheless, our evidence suggests that attitudes about taxes had become the most important political issue a full two years before Jarvis became a household word.

Next to a favorable image on taxes, the second most important image is whether the candidate is seen as "honest with the people and in speeches and promises."[29] This was clearly an issue that was an asset both to Carter and to Ford. Carter had based his whole campaign on being an outsider who was free of the taint of Watergate and corruption in government. In an age of declining trust in politicians, he presented himself as a peanut farmer from Georgia. He made a virtue of his lack of personal ties in his own Democratic party's establishment, some of whose members had brought the nation the Vietnam War and the credibility gap. As we have seen, Carter thereby created an image of integrity for himself, and convinced one-fifth of our respondents that he was more honest than President Ford. Ford himself was seen as a decent man whose greatest accomplishment as president was perhaps to restore some moral stature to the office that had been

Figure 5.6 Best Predictors of 1976 Presidential Vote*

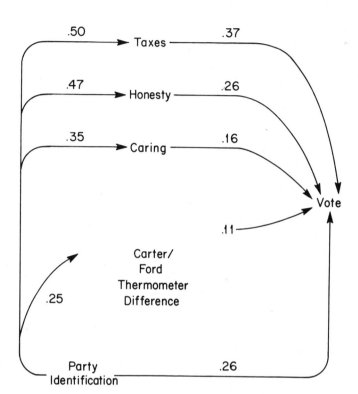

Variable	Effects		
	Direct	Indirect Impact Through Other Variables	Total
Party I.D.	.26	.40	.66
Taxes	.37		.37
Honesty	.26		.26
Caring	.16		.16
Carter-Ford Thermometer	.11		.11

* $R^2 = 76$ (N=113)

so tainted by Lyndon Johnson's tragic conduct of the war in Vietnam and by Richard Nixon's personal involvement in the Watergate affair. President Ford convinced two-fifths of our respondents that he was more honest than the peanut farmer from Georgia.

This concern with honesty is understandable as one looks back on the last few decades of the presidency. Truman and Eisenhower, each in his own way, were considered above reproach by most Americans on this score. The Kennedy administration ushered in a new mood, however. President Kennedy's dramatic rhetoric earned him a reputation in many circles as a leader who promised more than he could deliver, and who therefore created both a revolution of rising expectations and a cynical disappointment in those who did not see their promised dreams fulfilled. President Johnson's explanations of his Vietnam policy outraged his numerous critics, who added the phrase "credibility gap" to our language. Richard Nixon then succeeded to the presidency under such a moral cloud from his own previous political behavior that he was forced to promise the American people that he was "a new Nixon." Whatever tentative hopes they may have held that this was true were dashed to unprecedented depths by his near impeachment for criminal activity and the realization that he had lied to the American public and to the Congress. With such a legacy, one can understand the importance voters attached to honesty in the 1976 campaign.

The third image is caring more for the common people. This theme is much less important than the tax theme or the honesty theme. It is perhaps not surprising that Carter, as the Democratic nominee, scored higher on this image. As we have seen, the Democrats have traditionally been seen as the party of the common man. When we asked respondents how they felt different social and economic groups voted, the only ones seen as Republicans by a majority of respondents were conservatives and big businessmen. Republicans have struggled for over 40 years with an image as a party that caters to these special interests, to the detriment of the common man. What is surprising is that this theme of caring is not such a simple partisan issue after all. In fact, a glance at Figure 5.6 shows it is less influenced by partisanship than the image on taxes or the image of honesty. Who is perceived better at managing the economy, analyzed earlier in this chapter, is also more shaped by party identification than is the image of caring for the common man. Beyond partisanship, President Ford had convinced some Democrats that he cared more about the common man than Carter did, and Jimmy Carter convinced some Republicans that he cared more for the common man than President Ford did. And those voters, once convinced, sometimes voted against their party, just as those convinced on the taxes and honesty themes did.

It is worthy of note that even after the three themes of honesty, caring, and taxes had been added to party identification and thermometer ratings, there were still 5% to 10% of the respondents whose vote we could not accurately predict. In our effort to explain the rest of these voters' behavior, we found that the image of who is better at running the economy—Ford or Carter—was helpful. It explained a certain amount of additional votes. This additional amount was so fractional, however, that it did not alter the round numbers of 96% of Carter voters and 91% of Ford voters accurately accounted for, so we left this fourth image out of Figure 5.6 to keep the picture as simple, or parsimonious, as possible. Beyond that fourth image, no other variable made a significant contribution to explaining the election results.[30]

In this analysis of candidate images, we must not lose sight of the fact that party identification remains the dominant force in presidential voting. The panel data, as seen in chapter four, show that partisan attachments have been stable throughout the three-year period of the study. They existed long before the emergence of these image themes, and largely shape opinion on them. Party identification acting indirectly is the major determinant of voting behavior in the study, and the total (direct and indirect) impact of party is almost twice that of the tax theme.

In summary, we have an election dominated by party and image and devoid of 'issues' in the pure sense of that term. Beyond the effect of partisanship, it is hard to be certain what determined the vote. Our inductive path analysis suggested the pre-eminent importance of campaign images. We hesitate to yield the floor entirely to this point of view. The data on images were collected after the campaign and introduced in an inductive fashion. Our earlier analysis, which was more deductive, and which allowed a forecast of the election outcome from data collected in the primaries, shows the importance of evaluations of candidates' character in the voter's decision. Of course, while in the one analysis we focus on "images of the candidates" and in the other on "perceived character of the candidates," in either case we see that the voters were deciding first on the basis of party, second on their opinion of the candidates, and not at all on issues or ideology.[31] The 1976 national election study by Miller and Levitin similarly recognizes the importance of the personal attributes of the candidates.[32] But the Center for Political Studies questionnaire did not include *any* of the new questions with which we are able to document the specific dimensions of candidate appeal.

The reader, recalling our framework of candidate traits (Table 1.1) will note that two traits associated with the president's role as elected representative proved central to the election: honesty with the people and caring about the people. Also important were two images of issue-oriented competence: managing the economy and keeping down the costs of government. Other traits, including both general personal traits common to all human beings (e.g., intelligence or stupidity) and traits related to a specific presidential role (e.g., moral example) were less relevant, it would seem, to the election outcome. The relatively low importance of general personal traits (intelligence, reasonableness, strength, inspirational ability, and experience) is interesting because these traits are the least specifically political of those we studied. In that sense, they are traits that would be of concern to an electorate that had a very low awareness of politics. Almond and Verba distinguish three classes of political objects: roles, persons filling the roles, and policies.[33] A voter who judged candidates on only the second of these (personality) would be parochial with regard to policies and the structures of the system, and a participant only with regard to the personalities. Politics would be reduced to a "personality contest." The voters we studied seem more sophisticated. As we have seen, they believe that the candidates differ greatly on these general personality traits; yet the voting decisions are more highly correlated with the role-related and policy-related qualities of the candidates. The citizens seem sophisticated enough in their voting decisions to choose candidates who have (1) an image of being skilled in dealing with specific issues, and (2) an image of being caring and honest in dealings with the public. The voters do not, however, seem able to give the high marks for issue competence to the candidate whose stand is closest to theirs on the issue. Therefore, at least within the range of disagreement in 1976, issue positions remain insignificant to the voters, and images of competence can be won by candidates whose position on the issues differs from that of the voters.

We have noted the insignificance of issues and ideology in 1976. Indeed the items which did not work well in predicting the outcome in 1976 are, in many ways, as interesting as those which did. They include opinions on who is the more intelligent candidate; who is the better candidate for insuring peace; which political party is better for peace, for the economy, for the people, or for cutting waste in government; and the position of the voter on government income maintenance,

157

busing, post-materialism, women's liberation, and black militants. All these and more were added to the deductive model, and none of them succeeded in increasing its explanatory power. In short, (1) issue positions of the voters were not significant in 1976; (2) perceptions of party (as opposed to candidate) capabilities were not significant; and (3) while many candidate images mattered, those involving the candidates' intelligence and contributions to peace were not significant.

It may be that the media influenced the downplaying of issues. The instant analysis dished up by NBC, ABC, and CBS, while designed to be educational, focused so much on whose water glass had or hadn't spilled, and other questions of style and image, as to make the viewer repress or forget many prior observations about the issues.

Whatever these larger forces at work in the structure of the political system and the media, we are left with the observation that the 1976 presidential election outcome was determined by partisan habit and by opinions about the candidates, with issue differences reduced to a minor and insignificant role.

Predicting the Switch

Now that we have discussed the 1972 and 1976 elections separately, it is time to put our entire analysis into one package. Can we predict who will vote for the Republican's Presidential nominee *both* years? Can we predict who will vote consistently Democratic-for McGovern *and* for Carter? Can we predict who will vote for McGovern and then Ford? Most importantly, can we predict which voters will vote for Nixon in 1972 and then for Carter in 1976? To attempt this, we gathered the data from all four waves of our panel, and predicted votes with discriminant analysis, which is the technique (discussed earlier) for seeing what percentage of votes we can correctly guess, once we know voter attitudes and party identification.

Treating the switch from Nixon to Carter as a process, it is possible to successfully predict which voters will make the switch. The process is a two-step one in which voters first decide their 1972 vote and then decide their 1976 vote (Figure 5.7).

We predict their 1972 vote on the basis of their party identification, thermometer differences between Nixon and McGovern, and positions on post-materialism, busing, and women's liberation. Then, we predict their vote in 1976 on the basis of their party identification, and assessment of candidates' honesty, concern for the common man, and tax-minimizing skills. Dealing with the very small number of voters who

Figure 5.7 The Voting Process

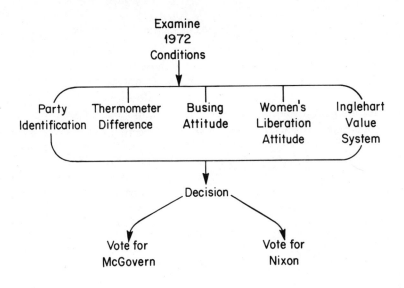

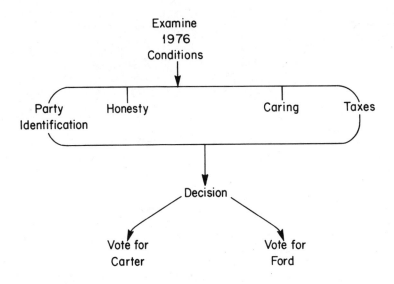

TABLE 5.26
Predicted and actual vote of panel survivors, with % of predictions correct.

		Prediction				
A C T U A L V O T E		Nixon-Ford	Nixon-Carter	McGovern-Ford	McGovern-Carter	Percent correct
	Nixon-Ford	54	1	5	4	84
	Nixon-Carter	0	10	0	6	63
	McGovern-Ford	2	0	3	1	50
	McGovern-Carter	0	2	2	28	88
	% correct	96	77	30	72	N=118

answered all these questions and remained in the panel, we predict how *118* people will vote, and we make a mistake with only *23* people (See Table 5.26). Treating the voters' decisions as a two-step process is necessary to producing such accurate predictions.

As we see in Table 5.26, predictions are best for the Nixon-Ford vote, where 96% of the votes are correctly predicted. This success is understandable, given that the Republican party was not cross-pressured or fractured by the turmoil of the social issues. In contrast, our predictions of persistent Democratic voting are correct 72% of the time, still respectable but reflecting the disruption of the times. We have about the same accuracy in predicting Nixon-Carter switchers; here we get 77% correct. It is interesting that we can predict these vote switchers fairly accurately with our model, but do not do quite as well predicting the McGovern-Ford switchers. The McGovern-Ford vote is not switching on the basis of the cross-cutting issues included in our model, so we have trouble accounting for them, and get only 30% of the predictions right. Overall, for 81% of the voters we have two correct predictions, both 1972 and 1976. For 16% of the voters, we correctly predicted one vote, either 1972 or 1976, but were wrong on the other. For 3% of the voters, our predictions in both years were wrong.

The accuracy of such predictions, however, must be weighed against a meaningful baseline. To successfully predict 60% of the people who voted for Lyndon Johnson in 1964 is not very impressive. Since 60% of the American voters voted for Johnson, one would be right 60% of the

160

time just by guessing that each voter voted for Johnson. On the other hand, to successfully predict 60% of those who would vote Socialist-Labor that year would be an impressive accomplishment, since they are so small in numbers that someone who was just guessing randomly in the general United States population would be lucky to find one Socialist-Labor voter in a thousand.

The baseline we use in evaluating our voter predictions is the percentage of voters who actually did vote a certain way. It is easy to get Nixon-Ford voters right, because of a high baseline, and hardest to get McGovern-Ford voters right, because they make up only 5% of the people in the table and hence have a low baseline. Looking at party voters, we successfully predicted 84% of the Nixon-Ford voters, an improvement over the 54% we would have gotten by random guessing, and 88% of the McGovern-Carter voters, a massive improvement over the 27% we would have gotten through random guessing. Looking at the switchers, we successfully predicted 63% of the Nixon-Carter voters; this is also a significant improvement over the 14% we would have gotten by random guessing. We also successfully predicted 50% of the McGovern-Ford voters, a considerable improvement over the 5% we would have gotten through random guesses.

CHAPTER 6: 1980 and Beyond

As mentioned in chapter one, Dearborn is just one city in the American north, but in many ways it is illustrative of what is happening elsewhere. Its attitudinal and voting patterns are close enough to national norms for us to believe that political trends here can give insight into what is happening elsewhere. On this basis we can assess the realignment process, prospects for the two-party system, and the condition of democracy in America's heartland.

The Sundquist Model: An Evaluation

The Sundquist model of partisan realignment is based upon a chain of events. It begins with an existing alignment perhaps three to four decades old, based on an outdated conflict. This *status quo* is broken by the emergence of powerful new problems and issues which cut across the political spectrum and polarize the community. Initially, party politicians have a natural aversion to such new unknown issues and will try to ignore them, but activist groups within each party force these issues to the forefront. If neither party takes up the new issue, a third party or movement may develop. At this point one of three things can happen: the third party can gain strength and replace one of the other parties; new issue activists can gain control of one of the weakened major parties and change its policies, thus producing a realignment; or new issue proponents can gain control of both major parties, thus producing no relative change in party balance. If a realignment does occur (either producing a new party or reinforcing the domination of the old major party) the minority party will gradually come to terms with the new reality and adjust.

The pattern described by Sundquist is remarkably close to the one seen in the United States since the mid-1960's, although with some noticeable differences. The New Deal alignment of Roosevelt, based

162

as it was on a philosophy of federal activism, saw a resurgence in the 1960's under Kennedy and Johnson, but just as it approached a peak in 1964, Barry Goldwater became the first presidential candidate to mention "crime in the streets," and George Wallace penetrated the north with a campaign based on opposition to federal intervention in the area of social relations. For various reasons—ideological preference and strategic advantage being two key ones—the minority Republicans were able to capture these issues more than the majority Democrats, who in 1968, and even more in 1972, were fragmented to a point of humiliation. At this point the parties were—according to the Sundquist model—tottering on the brink of realignment. The reasons they did not realign are only partially covered by the scenarios outlined in that model.

To start with, Sundquist's model de-emphasizes the possibility that the old issue can re-emerge as the most salient focus of voter concern. It seems to assume that issues are temporal and pass in the course of time, as slavery did. But some issues are the manifestation of fundamental cleavages in the polity. These cleavages ebb and flow with the events of the day but are seldom far below the surface. The prosperity of the 1950's and 1960's reduced the salience of the New Deal dimension but did not eliminate it. The sluggish economy between 1969 and 1972 nearly upended the Nixon presidency. Polls at the beginning of 1972 showed him neck and neck with Senator Muskie, then considered the likely Democratic nominee. Only a massive pump-priming effort was able to nullify the cleavage and allow other dimensions—peace and war, the social issue, personal competence—to play a major role in the 1972 election. The 1973 recession, partially a result of the stop-gap economic policies of 1972, re-established the economic cleavage as a dominant one in the 1976 election.

The impact of this re-emergence is not seen so much in issue attitudes (as one would suspect from the model) as in the relevance of partisanship, and here we see a second weakness in the model. V. O. Key, who wrote on realignments, suggested that for 'rational' voting to occur, the voters had to be aware of the issues and of the different positions of the parties. What our analysis suggests is that while many voters are indeed well informed, the party label serves as a summary of ideological positions and historical cleavage for others. Like a salmon which knows that in a certain season it must return to its home but does not quite know why, the voter, in times of crisis, may not understand all the issues but may feel that it is better to stay close to the

163

home party until tensions abate. The Sundquist model posits for conceptual reasons a perfect information condition with free floating voters and with partisanship as a dependent variable. In fact party identification over time is fairly stable and in reality only a moderate proportion of voters are what we would call well informed. The persisting power of the party as an independent variable in the political process is an element which we feel needs to be emphasized.

A third pattern which is somewhat at variance with Sundquist is the fact that one set of issues did not replace the others but co-existed with them in the political sphere. Rather than replacement, we prefer to emphasize the term salience. The relative decline of the New Deal dimension in the later 1960's and early 1970's did not mean that these issues were dead, just as the emergence of the 'social issue' during the same time did not suggest that it had replaced the previous cleavage. Going a step further, the decline of the social issue in the 1976 election does not mean that the issue dimension is dead. On the contrary, our data show it is strong and persistent.

The implications of this dual dimension-shifting salience pattern is that realignment is less likely than disruption. Unpredictability and wild fluctuations in party fortunes are more likely than the replacement of one party with another or the establishment of a new majority. The replacement model posits stability, buffeted only by realignments every 40 years or so. Our modification posits the possibility of instability, mixed with occasional periods of old issue salience when the majority party will be temporarily restored to its golden age of dominance.

A fourth modification we would suggest in the Sundquist model is that it take into account candidate images as a variable. Sundquist assumes that voters shift on the basis of issues. We would suggest that voters also shift on the basis of perception of candidate personalities and competencies in dealing with themes debated in the campaign. In the presence of confusing issues and in the absence of clear alternatives, voters may opt for the candidate who *seems* best able to restore order, promote prosperity, secure peace, and personify the fundamental values of the nation. In 1976, for example, we are hard pressed to find any *issue* which made a true difference in the outcome. Instead, we find that voters based their votes on party (identification), and candidate evaluation (both in terms of competence in handling key problems, and in personal integrity). Such a system is very hard to realign because issue position is not relevant to candidate preference, nor is issue position closely tied to partisan identity.

The Future of American Politics

There are several conclusions which are clearly supportable by our data. To start with, there is no evidence of a rapid realignment. Party identifications remain strong; the New Deal dimension remains salient and linked to partisanship; both parties have clear cut support groups who oppose each other in philosophical and practical ways which make compromise unlikely; the images of the parties and their perceived policy directions remain as distinct as their support groups. Those prophets of doom who project past Republican declines into the future and conclude that the party is terminal are not being realistic. Like-wise, those who project the disintegration of the Democratic party into distinct entities overlook the basic philosophical consensus which exists throughout much of the party on key issues.

What we do see is two weakened parties, whipsawed by issues and events, no longer able to rely upon party identifiers to support candidates out of simple loyalty. The basis of party defection, as revealed by our analysis, is an absence of overlap between party identification, policy preference on salient issues, and perceived candidate performance capabilities. As perceived capabilities shift according to circumstances, and as issue salience shifts (from social welfare to peace to social relationships to jobs), the voter is forced to reassess parties and candidates in an effort to maximize his preferences.

A question of concern to us and to other political scientists is whether this voter shift is based on ephemeral image manipulation made possible by voter ignorance and apathy, or whether it represents a more "rational" thrust. Democracy as an ideal is a system in which voters are informed, and vote on the basis of their issue preferences for candidates who will carry out those preferences. We found citizens who were far from this ideal: they did not always have accurate political information; they did not know where they themselves stood on many issues; they were often not clear about where candidates stood; and they did not always vote for candidates close to them. But these imperfections have been documented repeatedly since the first voting studies in the 1930's, and they come as no surprise. Some political scientists have suggested that such human lapses are to be expected, and that a more realistic theory of democracy is more appropriate for understanding democratic government in action. Downs, for example, has suggested that a functioning democracy is one where competing parties present critical alternatives to voters for decision. The voters chose one party or the other to carry out its campaign platform. Such a

165

model of responsible party government assumes a political system in which voter issue preferences shape the choice of a political party.

Our results indicate that even this watered-down model of democracy does not fully describe the system we observed. In 1972, voters who broke from their Democratic allegiance to vote for Nixon were well-informed and were motivated to vote for a candidate closer to them on the salient cross-cutting issues. This is in accord with a model of responsible party government in which voters switch to the party closest to them on the issues. However, the 1976 election was much less issue-oriented than that of 1972, and the 1976 return to the New Deal alignment can be explained largely by party identification without support of the issues that once provided the logic behind that identity.

On the positive side, however, we find that most voters have a functional or better level of information about the parties, candidates, and issues. Furthermore, when looking at those voters who shifted from party to party in their presidential vote, we find them well-informed and issue-oriented. Perhaps most impressively, we find that when we program into the computer the key concerns discussed in chapter five, our ability to explain voting patterns by the use of predictable and logical variables is very high. While we are concerned about the impact of media manipulation and apathy on political integration, we nevertheless see a strong element of rational preference manifested in the behavior of our respondents.

Nevertheless, one should not confuse rationality with stability. Those two would only go together in the presence of some sort of a consensus or at least majority position. In fact, insofar as we can determine, public opinion remains divided by the presence of two divisive issue-dimensions which do not overlap and hence have a strong disruption potential. The parties, for their part, are not able to heal this division. We can expect the future to hold what the past has seen: electoral upsets, party disruptions, voter anger, extra-party movements, and insurgent challenges to party leaderships.

Finally, we see party and candidate images playing an increasingly important role as determinants of voting behavior. While images have always played some role, their contemporary prominence is what is so notable. The reason for this prominence is not clear, but perhaps lies in sources not measurable by opinion surveys—the role of the media, for example. Other factors such as the complexity of issues and the policy-unreliability of the past few presidents may have led the voters to a certain distrust in issue statements.

In any case, politics in the future are definitely going to be different

166

from politics in the past. We complete this study with some apprehension, but at least the feeling that whatever comes will not be too unexpected. It is only appropriate that we end by allowing three of our respondents to tell you how they felt about the events of the era. Immediately after the election, we contacted people for the fourth and final time and asked them "Is there any comment you might like to make about this election or about either of the candidates which would help us understand how you feel about what happened?"

One respondent said, "I'd like to finish eating my chicken." A second said, "I don't vote because I am more interested in the Bible and the Lord than in politics." A third, a Ford supporter, said, "I was very delighted about voter turnout. This is the democratic process that people died for. Now we will have to wait and see what happens."

Indeed we will.

APPENDIX A: Study Design

This study uses a panel design, that is, it is constructed to observe attitude change by reinterviewing the same respondents repeatedly. For the first wave, several hundred heads of household were selected from the *Polk City Directory*. Eighty percent of those actually living at the indicated addresses were contacted and interviewed in February and March of 1974. Respondents were asked a broad battery of questions on items that might affect their partisanship and their vote in November 1976 (see Appendix B). In February and March of 1975, respondents were reinterviewed, with many questions repeated, and several new questions added. A new control group was also interviewed. The new names were drawn from the *Bresser's City Directory*. The responses of this group were compared with the responses of the reinterviewed group. Differences could be due to (1) bias introduced by panel mortality, panel learning, and other contamination, (2) changes in the Dearborn population from 1974 to 1975, the years when the two city directories were produced, (3) differences in the data collection techniques of Polk and Bresser, and (4) sample error. The static quality of Dearborn residential patterns led us to discount the second factor, and the similarity of listings and methods of data gathering led us to discount the third. Since the major differences between the two groups centered on the fact that the reinterviewed respondents were better informed and more Republican, we concluded that the differences could be largely attributed to the first factor.

A third wave of interviews was conducted in February and March of 1976, just after the New Hampshire primary. Of the 801 people who had been interviewed in 1974 and/or 1975, 416 (52%) were reinterviewed. This third wave contained the longest questionnaire, because new questions were asked about issues, parties and potential presidential nominees.

In November, 1976, a post-election interview was conducted to see

168

how respondents had voted. This fourth wave completed the study. To insure a high response rate (59% of the 801 respondents participated in this wave), the questionnaire was shortened. It had already been determined that little true change was occurring in the attitudes measured in the study, and a decision was made not to try to measure attitude change further by reasking the same questions. Hence, the fourth wave is of limited utility to those interested in attitude change. What the fourth wave does provide is a measure of our dependent variable—how people voted in 1976.

Wave I February 1974	Wave II February 1975	Wave III March 1976	Wave IV November 1976
Respondents N = 451*	Old Respondents (Survivors of 1974 Wave) N = 278 (61% of 451)	Pre-Primary Respondents (Survivors of 1974 and/or 1975 Wave)	Post-General Election Respondents
	New Respondents N = 350* (Control Group for Panel Bias)		
	Total N = 628	N = 416 (52% of 801)	N = 472 (59% of 801)

*First time interview rate was over 80% in both years.

APPENDIX B: Questionnaire

The following questions were asked of respondents. After each item, the Roman numeral indicates the wave (I = February/March 1974; II = February/March 1975; III = March/April 1976; Wave IV items are listed separately at the end of the Appendix).

1. Let's start out with a very general question. Of all the problems facing this country, what would you say is the *single most serious*. Just one. The most important of all? What would you say is the second most important? Is there a third one which you would want to mention?

    (I, II, III)

2. There are many groups in America that try to get the government or the American people to see things more their way. We would like to get your feelings towards some of these groups. I have here a card on which there is something that looks like a thermometer. We call it a "feeling thermometer" because it measures your feelings towards groups.

    Here's how it works. If you don't know too much about a group, or don't feel particularly warm or cold towards them, then you should place them in the middle, at the 50° mark.

    If you have a warm feeling toward a group, or feel favorably toward it, you would give it a score somewhere between 50° and 100°, depending on how warm your feeling is toward the group. On the other hand, if you don't feel very favorably toward some of these groups—if there are some you don't care for too much—then you would place them somewhere between 0° and 50°.

    Are you ready to begin?
    1. big business   (I, II, III)
    2. liberals   (I, II, III)
    3. Catholics   (I, II)

4. policemen	(I, II, III)
5. young people	(I, II)
6. Democrats	(I, II, III)
7. whites	(I, II, III)
8. Jews	(I, II)
9. labor unions	(I, II, III)
10. black militants	(I, II, III)
11. Republicans	(I, II, III)
12. homosexuals	(I, II, III)
13. school teachers	(I, II)
14. Protestants	(I, II)
15. blacks	(I, II, III)
16. conservatives	(I, II, III)
17. politicians	(I, II, III)
18. the women's lib movement	(I, II, III)
19. marijuana users	(I, II, III)
20. the military	(I, II)
21. urban rioters	(I, II)

Now here are a few national political figures. We would like to get your feelings toward them.

1. Spiro Agnew	(I)
2. George McGovern	(I)
3. Ronald Reagan	(I, II, III)
4. Richard Nixon	(I)
5. Edward Kennedy	(I, II, III)
6. Sam Ervin	(I)
7. George Wallace	(I, II, III)
8. Gerald Ford	(I, II, III)
9. Henry Jackson	(II, III)
10. Nelson Rockefeller	(II, III)
11. Hubert Humphrey	(III)
12. Jimmy Carter	(II, III)
13. Morris Udall	(II, III)
14. Charles Percy	(II, III)

3. In an election, such as for governor or senator, the parties will offer candidates and the public will choose among them. In such an election, some people vote for the *political party* they support. Others base their vote on what the candidates say about *political issues*. Still others vote for the candidate whom they believe has the best character. What do you most often base your vote on?

171

1. political party label
2. the candidate's position on issues, or
3. the candidate's character

(I, II)

4. Some persons say that news reporting is biased. Others feel that news reports are truthful . . . would you say that the news you read and hear is mostly:
    1. truthful and accurate *or*
    2. biased and one-sided

(I, II, III)

5. Do you think the theaters in Dearborn should show X-rated films, or should ban X-rated films?

(I, II, III)

6. Do you feel that capital punishment (that is, executing criminals for certain serious crimes) should be stopped or continued?

(I, II, III)

7. Would you be willing to pay more taxes to reduce pollution?

(I, II, III)

8a. If you had to choose among the following things, which are the two that seem most desirable to you?
    A. maintaining order in the nation
    B. giving the people more say in important political decisions
    C. fighting rising prices
    D. protecting freedom of speech

(First Set: Post-Bourgeois)

(I, III)

8b. Which of those is *most* important?

(I, III)

8c. I have one more list of goals for this country. If you had to choose among the following, which are the two that seem most desirable to you?
    E. Maintain a stable economy
    F. The fight against crime
    G. Move toward a friendlier, less impersonal society
    H. Move toward a society where ideas are more important than money

(Second Set: Self-actualization)

(I, II)

8d. Which of those is most important?

(I, II)

9. Many blacks are interested in getting better jobs and in gaining respect in their communities. What advice would *you* give them to achieve these goals?

(I)

10. The black unemployment rate in the U.S. is almost twice the unemployment rate for white persons. Which of the following would you say *best* explains this?
    1. most blacks are less reliable than whites
    2. blacks are discriminated against when applying for jobs, even when qualified
    3. a lack of skills among blacks due to poor training
    4. lack of skills among blacks due to slowness to learn and low motivation

(I, II, III)

I will read some statements to you and all you have to do is tell me whether you agree or disagree. If you are not sure of how you feel, just tell me which way you think you lean. Remember there are no correct answers. I simply want your opinion.

11. Every American has a right to own a gun and should not be required to register it.

(I, II, III)

12. I don't think public officials care much about what people like me think.

(I, II, III)

13. Any group, no matter how radical its views, should be allowed to march and protest government policy, so long as there is no violence.

(I, II)

14. Both major parties in this country are controlled by small groups of men and are run for their benefit.

(I, II, III)

15. There is no use worrying my head off about public affairs; I can't do anything about them anyway.

(I, II, III)

16. Every woman should have the right to an abortion if she wants one.

(I, II, III)

17. Voting is the only way that people like me can have any say about how the government runs things.

(I, II)

18. A man who doesn't know what he is talking about shouldn't be allowed to speak.

(I, II)

19. The government ought to help people get doctors and hospital care at low cost.

(I, II, III)

20. People like me don't have any say about how the government runs things.

(I, II, III)

21. Sex education is a private matter. It should *not* be taught in the schools.

(I, II, III)

22. Most politicians can be trusted to do what they think is best for the country.

(I, II, III)

23. Sometimes politics and government seem so complicated that a person like me can't really understand what's going on.

(I, II, III)

24. The government in Washington ought to see to it that everybody who wants to work can find a job.

(I, II, III)

25. The government ought to make sure that all people have a good standard of living.

(I, II, III)

26. Many judges are too soft on criminals.

(I, II)

27. Anyone who can't afford adequate housing should be able to get a loan from the government.

(I, II, III)

28. A school should have the right to fire a teacher who lets his hair grow too long.

(I, II)

29. The government should not feel obliged to give loans to poor students.

(I, II, III)

30. Police should be allowed to search or question a suspicious person without having to worry about his rights.

(I, II, III)

31. While there may be exceptions, most women are better off working in the home.

(III)

32. No American should be allowed to own a handgun, such as a pistol.

(III)

33. My impression is that most government agencies are not nearly as efficient as the average private company or business.

(III)

34. The government is trying to do too many things to help people. The country would be better off if many of these programs were ended.

(III)

35. Some school systems have begun busing students from schools in black areas of the city to schools which have many white students. What is your opinion of the busing of students from one area to another?
    1. I strongly favor it
    2. I favor it
    3. I oppose it
    4. I strongly oppose it

(I, II, III)

36. In the United States, there have been many marriages between a black and a white person . . . what would you say are your feelings toward such marriages?
    1. they are purely a personal matter and I have no objection
    2. I disapprove but feel that it is none of my business
    3. I do not object but feel that a person should think carefully before entering such a marriage
    4. I feel they are morally wrong

(I, II, III)

37. Have you ever watched the TV show, All in the Family, with Archie Bunker and Meathead?

(I)

38. In that show, do you tend to agree more with the opinions expressed by Archie Bunker, or with those expressed by Archie's son-in-law, Meathead?

(I)

39. Some people have pointed out that many grade schools and high schools are not of very good quality. Generally richer neighborhoods have better schools and poorer neighborhoods have poorer schools. Would you favor a proposal to have the government give each school an equal amount of money for each child so that the schools would be more equal?

(III)

40. Suppose your party nominated a qualified woman for president. Would you be inclined to vote for her or against her?

(III)

41. In the last few months have you heard mostly good news or mostly bad news about the economy?

(III)

42. Here is a list of groups which are important in the American economy. Which of these groups do you think is *most* responsible for the difficulties which our economy is today experiencing?
    1. big corporations
    2. labor unions
    3. the Republicans
    4. the Democrats
    5. foreigners, like the Arabs
    6. the Military
    7. the American people themselves
    8. other (explain)

43. Many people feel that to reduce racial tension in this country, we should encourage blacks and whites to live together in the same neighborhoods. Others argue that it is better for people to live among their own kind. If the people who wanted mixed neighborhoods were at one end of this scale—at point one—and the people who wanted separate neighborhoods were at the other end—at point seven—
    a. Where would you place yourself?
    b. Where would you place Gerald Ford?

  c. Where would you place the Republican Party?
  d. Where would you place the Democratic Party?
  e. Where would you place (favorite Democrat)?

(II, III)

44. Some people feel that the government in Washington should see to it that every person has a job and a good standard of living. Others think the government should just let each person get ahead on his own. And, of course, other people have opinions somewhere in between. Suppose people who believe that the government should see to it that every person has a good standard of living are at one end of this scale—at point number one. And suppose that the people who believe that the government should let each person get ahead on his own are at the other end—at point number seven.

  a. Where would you place yourself on this scale, or haven't you thought much about this?
  b. Where would you place Gerald Ford on this scale?
  c. Where would you place the Republican party on this scale?
  d. Where would you place the Democratic Party?
  e. Where do you think (favorite Democrat) would be on this scale?

(II)

45. Some people feel that the government in Washington should guarantee each American a job, even if it has to create those jobs. Others think it is up to the individual to find a job in the free enterprise system. Suppose those people who wanted the government to create government jobs were at one end of this scale—at point one—and the people who wanted the free enterprise system to provide those jobs without government involvement were at the other end—at point seven. Where would you be on this scale, or haven't you thought about it?

  a. Where do you think Gerald Ford would go on this scale?
  b. Where would you place the Republican party?
  c. Where would you place the Democratic party?
  d. Where would you place (favorite Democrat)?

(III)

46. As you know, in our tax system people who earn a lot of money have to pay higher taxes than those who earn less. Some people

177

think that those with high incomes should pay even more than they do now. Others think that such people already pay enough. Suppose the people who want the rich to pay more are at one end of this scale—at point one—and those who think the rich already pay enough are at the other end—at point seven.

    a. Where would you place yourself on this scale, or haven't you thought much about this?

    b. Where would you place Gerald Ford on this scale?

    c. Where would you place the Republican Party?

    d. Where would you place the Democratic Party?

    e. Where would you place (favorite Democrat)?

(II)

47. There is much concern about the rapid rise in the medical and hospital costs. Some people feel there should be a government insurance plan which would cover all medical and hospital expenses. Others feel that medical expenses should be paid by individuals, and through private insurance like Blue Cross.

Suppose that all the people who wanted a government insurance program were at one end of this scale—at point one—and all the people who wanted individuals to arrange their own health insurance were at the other end—at point seven.

    a. Where would you place yourself on this scale, or haven't you thought much about this?

    b. Where would you place Gerald Ford on this scale?

    c. Where would you place the Republican party?

    d. Where would you place the Democratic party?

    e. Where would you place (favorite Democrat)?

(II, III)

48. There is much discussion about the best way to deal with racial problems. Some people think achieving racial integration of schools is so important that it justifies busing children to schools out of their own neighborhoods. Others think letting children go to their neighborhood schools is so important that they oppose busing.

Suppose all the people who want to integrate schools by busing children were at one end of this scale—at point one—and all the people who wanted to keep children in neighborhood schools were at the other end—at point seven.

    a. Where would you place yourself on this scale, or haven't you thought much about this?

b. Where would you place Gerald Ford on this scale?

c. Where would you place the Republican party?

d. Where would you place the Democratic party?

e. Where would you place (favorite Democrat)?

(II, III)

49. Many people have suggested that some of the economic problems of the country are caused by the unwillingness of the government to regulate business and industry; other people argue that the problem is too much regulation. Suppose the people who felt there was too much regulation were at one end of this scale—at point one—and those who felt there was too little regulation were at the other end—at point seven.

a. Where would you place yourself on this scale, or haven't you thought much about this?

b. Where would you place Gerald Ford on this scale?

c. Where would you place the Republican party?

d. Where would you place the Democratic party?

e. Where would you place (favorite Democrat)?

(II)

50. In the past few years the government has required that automobile companies put pollution control devices on their cars. Some people have argued that until the economy gets better, no new regulations should be added. Other people argue that these new regulations are very important and should continue as scheduled. Suppose the people who want to put off new regulations until the economy improves are at one end of this scale—at point one—and that those who want to continue with the regulations are at the other end—at point seven.

a. Where would you place yourself on this scale, or haven't you thought much about this?

b. Where would you place Gerald Ford on this scale?

c. Where would you place the Republican party?

d. Where would you place the Democratic party?

e. Where would you place (favorite Democrat)?

(II)

51. Some people have argued that the oil companies are so important to the economy that the government should take them over and run them, of course paying the owners for their property. Other people say the oil industry should be run by private enterprise. Suppose the people who want the government to run the

oil companies were at one end of this scale—at point one—and the people who want private enterprise to run the oil companies were at the other end—at point seven.

    a. Where would you place yourself on this scale, or haven't you thought much about this?
    b. Where would you place Gerald Ford on this scale?
    c. Where would you place the Republican party?
    d. Where would you place the Democratic party?
    e. Where would you place (favorite Democrat)?

(II)

52. We also hear a lot of talk about liberals and conservatives in this country. Look at this scale once again and imagine that those who call themselves liberals were at one end of this scale—at point one—and those who call themselves conservatives were at the other end—at point seven.

    a. Where would you place yourself on this scale?
    b. Where would you place Gerald Ford on this scale?
    c. Where would you place the Republican party?
    d. Where would you place the Democratic party?
    e. Where would you place (favorite Democrat)?

(II, III)

53. I would like to ask you a few questions about names and events in the news. We have intentionally chosen questions that most people can't answer, so if you don't know the answer, don't feel bad; we will just go on to another question.

    1. What is the capital of North Vietnam? (I)
    2. Who is the governor of Michigan? (I, II)
    3. Who are the two U.S. senators from Michigan? (I, II)
    4. Who is the congressional representative from this district? (I, II)
    5. Do you happen to remember how long a U.S. senator's term is? How long does he serve before he has to run for re-election? (I, II)
    6. Do you know who is the U.S. Secretary of State? (I)
    7. Do you know the name of the mayor of Dearborn? (I)
    8. Who is the vice president of the United States? (II)

    9. Do you know who is the Chief Justice of the U.S. Supreme Court? (II)

    10. Do you know the name of the mayor of Detroit? (II)

54. I would now like to read you a list of several presidential candidates. We are trying to find out how well known these candidates are. When I read a name to you, would you tell me the state from which that candidate comes. If you don't know, don't feel badly; many other people don't know either.

    1. George Wallace
    2. Gerald Ford
    3. Ted Kennedy
    4. Birch Bayh
    5. Jimmy Carter
    6. Morris Udall
    7. Edmund Muskie
    8. Henry Jackson
    9. Howard Baker
    10. Ronald Reagan

(III)

55a. On February 24, the United States had its first presidential primary of the 1976 race. Do you happen to remember the state in which that primary was held?

(III)

(IF THE ANSWER IS NOT NEW HAMPSHIRE, TELL IT WAS N.H.)

55b. Do you happen to remember the Democrat who got the most votes in that primary?

(III)

55c. Do you happen to remember the Republican who got the most votes in that primary?

(III)

56. Generally, do you consider yourself a Democrat, a Republican, or what?
(IF RESPONDENT SAYS "INDEPENDENT" SAY . . .)
Many people who are Independent tend to lean toward one party or the other. Would you say you are an Independent leaning toward the Republicans or an Independent leaning toward the Democrats?

(I, II, III)

57a. Five years ago, would you have answered that question the same, or have you changed your opinion since then?

(I, II)

57b. Five years ago, would you have been more inclined toward the Democrats than now, or more inclined towards the Republicans than now?

(I, II)

58. Do you recall your father's party? Was he a Republican or a Democrat?

(I, II)

59. The Democratic and Republican parties in this country some-times try to attract whole groups of people to support them. Let me read you some types of people. As you see it, do you think these people are *more likely* to be in the Democratic party or the Republican party?
    1. big business
    2. liberals
    3. Catholics
    4. policemen
    5. young people
    6. whites
    7. Jews
    8. labor union members
    9. black militants
    10. homosexuals
    11. school teachers
    12. protestants
    13. blacks
    14. conservatives
    15. women's lib advocates
    16. marijuana users
    17. member of the military
    18. urban rioters

(I, II)

60. Remember in 1968 when Hubert Humphrey, Richard Nixon and George Wallace were running for president? Did you vote in that election?

(I, II)

61. (IF YES) Who did you vote for—Humphrey, Nixon or Wallace?

(I, II)

62. Did you vote in the 1972 presidential election?

(I, II)

63. (IF YES) Which candidate did you vote for in that election?

(I, II)

64. Now, suppose the Democrats and the Republicans both nominated good candidates for president in 1976. The way you feel now, would you be more inclined to vote for the Democratic candidate or the Republican candidate?

(II, III)

65. A lot of people have said that there is no real difference between the Democratic and the Republican parties. From your point of view, what do you think are the main differences between these parties, or do you agree that there is no difference between them?

(II, III)

66. One of the big problems faced by the American government is maintaining world peace. In general, do you feel that the Democratic party or the Republican party is better able to promote world peace, or is there no difference between the parties in that area?

(II, III)

67. What about the matter of promoting prosperity and keeping the American economy healthy? Would you say the Republicans or Democrats are better able to do that, or is there no difference between the parties?

(II, III)

68. Which of the parties is better able—in the long run—to help people such as yourself, or is there no difference between them?

(III)

69. Which party do you feel is better able to cut out waste and inefficiency in government, or do you feel there is no real difference between them in this area?

(III)

70. Later this year America must choose a president. Here is a list of possible candidates from both parties. Which of these people—just one, either a Democrat or a Republican—would you *most* like to see elected president in 1976?

   Democrats
   1. Birch Bayh
   2. Jimmy Carter

3. Hubert Humphrey
4. Henry Jackson
5. Edward Kennedy
6. Edmund Muskie
7. Sargent Shriver
8. Morris Udall
9. George Wallace
    Republicans
1. Howard Baker
2. John Connally
3. Gerald Ford
4. Charles Percy
5. Ronald Reagan
6. Elliot Richardson
7. Nelson Rockefeller

(III)

71. Who is your second choice? Again just one name.

(III)

72. Of course we don't know who the candidates will be in November, but many people believe Gerald Ford will be the Republican nominee. The way you feel today, do you think you will be likely to vote for Gerald Ford or against him?

(III)

73. Who, of all these candidates, would you absolutely *not* want to see elected president in 1976? Again just one name.

(III)

74. Is there anyone else that you would *not* want to see elected?

(III)

75. Ignoring for a moment such things as position on the issues or party, which presidential candidate seems to you the most appealing and pleasant as a person?

(III)

76. Is there any presidential candidate that you find particularly unpleasant or unappealing as a person, again ignoring such things as position on the issues or party?

(III)

(THE NEXT FIVE QUESTIONS WERE ASKED IN 1976 ONLY. THEY WERE ASKED ABOUT THE FOLLOWING CANDI-

DATES: GERALD FORD, RONALD REAGAN, EDWARD KEN-
NEDY, JIMMY CARTER, AND GEORGE WALLACE.)

77. Now we would like to get your feelings about some of the candi-
     dates as people—what you think about their personalities and
     qualifications for the presidency.
     I will read you a trait such as whether the candidate seems
     experienced for the presidency—and then you will simply tell
     me if you feel that the candidate is experienced, very experi-
     enced, inexperienced, or very inexperienced. If you don't really
     know much about the candidate or don't have an opinion just
     tell me and we will go on to the next item. Are you ready to
     begin? Let's start with how much experience the candidates
     seem to have.

78. Now we'd like you to judge the strength of each candidate as a
     person. When I read you a candidate's name, tell me whether he
     strikes you as very strong, strong, weak, or very weak. If you
     don't have a feeling about a particular candidate, just say so and
     we'll go on.

79. Some candidates come across as inspiring leaders, and others
     seem just plain dull. When I read a candidate's name, tell me
     whether he strikes you as very inspiring, inspiring, dull or very
     dull.

80. Some candidates seem to propose ideas that are risky and dan-
     gerous, while others seem to stick to more sensible ideas. When
     I read a candidate's name, I'd like you to tell me whether you
     think of him as very sensible, sensible, risky, or very risky.

81. Finally, how about the moral leadership of the candidates?
     When I read a candidate's name, tell me whether you think he
     sets a good example for young people, a very good example, a
     poor example, or a very poor example.

82. Look at this ladder. It has ten rungs on it. Imagine that people
     were standing on that ladder, with the most happy people on the
     tenth rung and the least happy people on the first rung. Where
     would you place yourself on that ladder?

                                                          (I, II, III)

83. Where were you on that ladder five years ago?

                                                          (I, II, III)

84. Where do you think you will be five years from now?

                                                          (I, II, III)

85. People often talk about different social classes. I wonder which of these terms best describes you: working class, middle class, or upper class?

(I, II)

86. In the past year, have you been laid off or unemployed or otherwise out of work, except for reasons of illness?

(II, III)

(THE FOLLOWING WERE ASKED THE FIRST TIME THE RESPONDENT WAS INTERVIEWED)

87. How old are you?
88. What is your job, your occupation?
89. Do you own a home or are you renting?
90. What was the last grade of school you completed?
91. Are you a Protestant, Catholic, Jewish, or Moslem?
92. (IF PROTESTANT) What church is that?
93. Are you a member of a labor union or a trade union?
94. Here is a card showing different income groups. Give me the letter of the group your family is in.

(THE FOLLOWING WERE ASKED ONLY IN THE POST-ELECTION CALL-BACK)

95a. First, did you actually vote in the presidential election?
95b. Did you vote for Jimmy Carter or Gerald Ford or one of the other candidates?
96. What would you say was the main reason you decided to support (   )?
97. Now thinking back to last May when Michigan had its presidential primary election, do you remember if you voted in that election?
98a. Did you vote in the Democratic or the Republican primary?
98b. (IF VOTED IN DEMOCRATIC PRIMARY)
There were two active candidates in that race, Jimmy Carter and Morris Udall. Do you remember which of those you supported?
98c. (IF VOTED IN REPUBLICAN PRIMARY)
There were two candidates in that race, Gerald Ford and Ronald Reagan. Do you remember which of those you supported?
98d. (IF REMEMBERS VOTING BUT CAN'T REMEMBER WHICH PRIMARY)

Let me list for you all the candidates on the Michigan ballot and see which one you supported: On the Democratic side were Jimmy Carter and Morris Udall, as well as some non-active candidates such as George Wallace; on the Republican side were Gerald Ford and Ronald Reagan. Can you remember which of these you supported in the primary?

99.   There was a lot of talk during the campaign about which of the candidates was more intelligent. Did you consider Carter or Ford to be more intelligent or was there no different between them?

100.   What about being honest with the people in their speeches and promises? Was Carter or Ford more honest, or was there no difference?

101.   In terms of caring for the common people and their problems, did Carter or Ford seem more concerned?

102a.   Another issue in the campaign was keeping the economy healthy and solving the problems of unemployment and inflation. Which of the candidates seemed stronger on this point?

102b.   The economy has been suffering from two problems, unemployment and inflation. Which do you feel is the more serious?

103.   Another big campaign issue was the problem of maintaining world peace. Did Carter or Ford seem to be better able to do that?

104.   Finally, a lot of people were concerned about keeping down the cost of government and holding down taxes. From your point of view, was Carter or Ford better able to do this?

105.   Well, those are all the questions I have. Before I hang up, is there any comment you might like to make about this election or about either of the candidates which would help us understand how you feel about what happened?

Notes

Chapter 1

1. Everett Ladd, Jr., has documented the decline in support for institutional leaders. He finds massive declines in trust and respect over a ten year period, 1966–76. See "The Polls: The Question of Confidence," *Public Opinion Quarterly* 40 (Winter 1976–77), 544–552. The consequences of this new distrust are widely debated. One group of scholars, working under the auspices of the Trilateral Commission, wondered if it would be possible to continue to govern the United States. See Michel Crozier, Samuel Huntington, and Joji Watanuki, *The Crisis of Democracy* (New York: New York University Press, 1975). Note especially the section by Huntington on the United States, and the rebuttal by Ralf Dahrendorf in Appendix B.

2. Samuel Lubell provides a classic discussion of the development of the New Deal alignment. See *The Future of American Politics* (Garden City, New York: Doubleday Anchor, 1955).

3. Lubell, *The Future of American Politics,* p. 275.

4. The events of the 1972 campaign are ably chronicled in Theodore White, *The Making of the President 1972* (N.Y.: Atheneum Publishers, 1973).

5. See Kevin Phillips, *The Emerging Republican Majority* (New Rochelle, N.Y.: Arlington House, 1969).

6. The first systematic public opinion polling began in the early 1930's. See, for example, George Gallup, *The Gallup Poll 1935–1971* (New York: Random House, 1972). Samuel Stouffer's study of the American soldier, conducted during World War II, was a brilliant effort to test hypotheses using extensive individual-level survey data. See Samuel Stouffer, *et al., The American Soldier* (Princeton, N.J.: Princeton University Press, 1949). Pioneering studies of Presidential voting were carried out in 1944, both at the national level by the National Opinion Research Center at the University of Chicago, and at the local level in a classic community study. For the latter, see Paul Lazarsfeld, *The People's Choice* (N.Y.: Duell, Sloan, and Pierce, 1944).

7. V.O. Key, Jr., "A Theory of Critical Elections," *Journal of Politics* 17

(February 1955), 3–18. Key later qualified and modified his position somewhat in "Secular Realignments and the Party System," *Journal of Politics* 21 (May 1959), 198–210. Credit should also go to E.E. Schattschneider for his influential work, *The Semi-Sovereign People: A Realist View of Democracy.* (Hinsdale, Illinois: The Dryden Press, 1960).

8. Key, "A Theory of Critical Elections," pp. 4 and 11.

9. Key, "Secular Realignment and the Party System."

10. Angus Campbell, "A Classification of Presidential Elections," in Angus Campbell, *et al., Elections and the Political Order* (New York: John Wiley and Sons, 1966).

11. Everett Ladd with Charles Hadley, *Transformations of the American Party System: Political Coalitions from the New Deal to the 1970s* (N.Y.: W.W. Norton, 1970).

12. James Sunquist, *The Dynamics of the Party System* (Washington, D.C.: The Brookings Institution, 1973).

13. *Ibid.,* p. 9.

14. *Ibid.,* p. 279.

15. We commend to the readers an excellent essay by Richard Hofstadter which discusses the manner in which the complexities of trusts and high finance were reduced to basic ideological issues by the populists of the 1890s. See "Free Silver and the Mind of (Coin) Harvey," in Hofstadter, *The Paranoid Style in American Politics* (N.Y.: Vintage, 1967).

16. Sundquist, *Dynamics of the Party System,* p. 293.

17. Phillips, *The Emerging Republican Majority.*

18. Sundquist, *Dynamics of the Party System,* p. 293.

19. For a classic description of inheritance of party identification, see M. Kent Jennings and Richard Niemi, "The Transmission of Political Values from Parent to Child," *American Political Science Review* 62 (March 1968), 169–184. There is evidence that this transmission is on the decline, and this is discussed in Norman Nie, Sidney Verba, and John Petrocik, *The Changing American Voter* (Cambridge, Mass.: Harvard University Press, 1976), pp. 49, 70–73. For a recent study, see W. Phillips Shively, "The Development of Party Identification among Adults," *American Political Science Review* 73 (December 1979), 1039–1054.

20. Lubell, *The Future of American Politics,* p. 212.

21. Much of this discussion follows Sundquist, *Dynamics of the Party System.* Another excellent source is William Chambers and Walter Dean Burnham (eds.), *The American Party System: Stages of Political Development* (N.Y.: Oxford University Press, 1967), which goes back to the beginning of the Republic and focuses on five alignments (four realignments) instead of the four covered by Sundquist.

22. For a discussion of this party system, see Joel Silbey, *The Shrine of the Party: Congressional Voting Behavior, 1841–1852.* (Pittsburgh: University of Pittsburgh Press, 1967).

189

23. For a discussion of this realignment, see Sundquist, *The Dynamics of the Party System.*
24. Sundquist, *Dynamics of the Party System,* pp. 140–147.
25. For a different approach to the 1896 realignment, see Walter Dean Burnam, "The Changing Shape of the American Political Universe," *American Political Science Review,* 59 (March 1965), 7–28, and *Critical Elections and the Mainsprings of American Politics* (N.Y.: W.W. Norton, 1970). Burnam emphasizes economic change as a cause of the realignment, but also argues that the decreased competitiveness between the parties produced a decrease in working class participation in the political process. These issues are debated in Burnam's "Theory and Voting Research," as well as in the following "Comment" by Philip Converse and "Comment" by Jerrold Rusk, all in the *American Political Science Review,* 68 (September 1974), 1002–1057.
26. For a discussion of this realignment as measured in House of Representatives' voting patterns, see Barbara Sinclair, "Party Realignment and the Transformation of the Political Agenda: the House of Representatives, 1925–1938," *American Political Science Review,* 71 (September 1977), 940–953.
27. See Ladd with Hadley, *Transformations of the American Party System* for a discussion of post-New Deal party change at the grass-roots level. Ladd and Hadley show that social characteristics, such as social class, that affected voting in the New Deal era, have a much reduced and sometimes reversed effect on partisanship in the 1970s. This would suggest that predicting votes on the basis of ethnicity and class, as done by Robert Abelson, Ithiel Pool and Samuel Popkin, *Candidates, Issues and Strategies* (Cambridge, Mass.: M.I.T. Press, 1965) in the 1960 campaign, would no longer be useful. Ladd and Hadley also broaden the examination of party transformations beyond a focus on alignment and disintegration, and thereby rest their realignment discussion in a broader and very stimulating framework.
28. Robert Axelrod, "Where the Votes Come From: An Analysis of Electoral Coalitions, 1952–1972," in Jeff Fischel (ed.), *Parties and Elections in an Anti-Party Age* (Bloomington, Ind.: Indiana University Press, 1978), pp. 86–99.
29. In Norman Nie, Sidney Verba, and John Petrocik, *The Changing American Voter* (Cambridge, Mass.: Harvard University Press, 1979), enlarged edition, p. 11.
30. *Ibid.,* p. 233.
31. Ladd with Hadley, *Transformations of the American Party System.* The "anti-party age" is the topic of a useful reader by Fischel, *Parties and Elections in an Anti-Party Age.*
32. Ladd with Hadley, *Transformations of the American Party System,* pp. 26–27.

33. The case for a more responsible form of party government is made in the classic report, "Toward a More Responsible Two-Party System: A Report of the Committee on Political Parties, American Political Science Association," in the *American Political Science Review* (Supplement: Vol. 44, September 1959, Number 3, Part 2). For a reassessment of the report see Evron Kirkpatrick, "Toward a More Responsible Two Party System: Political Science, Policy Science, or Pseudo-Science," *American Political Review* 65 (December 1971), 965–990.
34. Ladd with Hadley, *Transformations of the American Party System*, pp. 337–338.
35. Starting with James Davies' attempts to measure the impact of charisma on the 1952 campaign, generations of scholars have had to code open-ended questions to get measures of leadership traits. This has made it difficult to treat personal qualities as more than random disturbances causing deviations from the normal impact of parties and issues on voting. For efforts to study the impact of personality by using open-ended questions, see James Davies, "Charisma in the 1952 Campaign." *American Political Science Review* 48 (December 1954): 1083–1102, and Benjamin Page and Calvin Jones, "Reciprocal Effects of Policy Preferences, Party Loyalities and the Vote," *American Political Science Review,* 73 (December 1979): 1071–1089. More recent studies have relied upon the feeling thermometer (described in chapter two). This measure is more empirically precise, but is too general to tell us about what makes a candidate appealing. Campbell, *et al., The American Voter* and *Elections and the Political Order* use both open-ended and closed ended questions. They also show as does Davies some association between lower levels of political conceptualization and candidate orientation.
36. Several scholars have written about presidential traits. Clinton Rossiter discussed presidential roles in *The American Presidency* (N.Y.: Mentor, 1960), revised edition; Thomas Cronin also discussed roles, more from a business-management perspective, in *The State of the Presidency* (Boston: Little, Brown, 1980), 155; James David Barber in *The Presidential Character* (Englewood Cliffs, N.J.: Prentice-Hall, 1977), focuses on personal-psychological orientations to power and their impact on leadership effectiveness; Richard Neustadt, *Presidential Power* (N.Y.: Signet, 1964), 23, speaks of "the power to persuade" as a critical trait; Erwin Hargrove in *Presidential Leadership* (N.Y.: Macmillan, 1966) shows that what appear to be positive qualifications or traits, such as moralism, can be counterproductive in office; Zbigniew Brzezinski and Samuel Huntington in *Political Power: USA-USSR* (N.Y.: Viking Press, 1964) speak of how alternative careers produce alternative types of qualities, some of them undesirable. For a summary of the social-psychological studies of leadership, see Cecil Gibb, "Leadership," in Gardner Lindzey and Elliot Aronson (eds.) *The Handbook of Social Psychology,* IV (Cambridge, Mass.: Addison-

Wesley, 1968), 268–273. For our purposes—the study of presidential selection—much of this social-psychological literature fails to put sufficient emphasis on the distinction between becoming a leader (election) and being a leader (governing). Lee Cronbach, *Essentials of Psychological Testing* (N.Y.: Harper and Row, 1970), 560–565, discusses psychological traits and the difficulty of limiting those to be studied. He discusses the "semantic differential" as a methodological technique, as do C. Osgood, *et al.*, in *The Measurement of Meaning* (Urbana, Illinois: University of Illinois Press, 1957). We use a modification of their semantic differential to study certain presidential image traits.

37. See Donald Anderson, "Presidential Availability: A Framework for Future Research," *Presidential Studies Quarterly* 8 (Fall 1978), 341–347. Anderson, in beginning to develop a theory of presidential selection, has drawn on the work of Sidney Verba and that of social psychologists. See Sidney Verba, *Small Groups and Political Behavior* (Princeton, N.J.: Princeton University Press, 1961). Our three-fold division of traits differs from that used by Anderson or Fred Lee, *Presidential Elite Support for the American Presidency* (Ph.D. dissertation, University of Michigan, 1978). Both Anderson and Lee dichotomize traits into instrumental and symbolic (or affective). Those categories probably cut across those we have developed.

38. Herbert Asher, *Presidential Elections and American Politics: Voters, Candidates and Campaigns since 1952* (Homewood, Ill.: Dorsey Press, 1976), pp. 312–314.

Chapter 2

1. The feeling thermometer was developed at the University of Michigan's Center for Political Studies for their 1968 election study. For an excellent discussion of what information is contained in the candidate feeling thermometer, see George Rabinowitz, *Spatial Models of Electoral Choice: An Empirical Analysis* (Chapel Hill, N.C.: University of North Carolina, Institute for Research in Social Science, 1973).

2. For a discussion of the causes and the implications of this trend, see Arthur Miller, "Political Issues and Trust in Government: 1964–1970," as well as the "Comment" by Jack Citrin and the "Rejoinder" by Arthur Miller, all in the *American Political Science Review,* 68 (September 1974), 951–1001.

3. Ronald Inglehart, "The Silent Revolution in Europe: Intergenerational Change in Post-Industrial Societies," *American Political Science Review* 65 (December 1971), 991–1017.

4. Abraham Maslow, *Motivation and Personality* (N.Y.: Harper and Row, 1970).

5. *Ibid.,* 39.

6. *Ibid.*, 45.
7. From Adams' letters to his wife, as quoted in John Bartlett, *Bartlett's Familiar Quotations* (Boston: Little, Brown and Company, 1968), 463.
8. See Ronald Inglehart, "Value Priorities, Subjective Satisfaction, and Protest Potential Among Western Publics," a paper delivered to the Annual Meeting of the American Political Science Association, San Francisco, California, September 1975. Alan Marsh's study of Britain confirms Inglehart's findings that post-materialists are younger, richer, and somewhat better educated than materialists. But Marsh's data raise questions about whether Inglehart has really measured Maslow's values. See Marsh's "The 'Silent Revolution,' Value Priorities, and the Quality of Life in Britain," *American Political Science Review*, 69 (March 1975), 21–30.
9. Ingelhart found this same pattern, even more dramatically. Ingelhart, "The Silent Revolution in Europe."
10. For a detailed discussion of the interactions between and among materialism, personal happiness, and income, see Ingelhart, "Value Priorities, Subjective Satisfaction and Protest Potential among Western Publics."
11. This technique was developed by Hadley C. Cantril in *The Pattern of Human Concerns* (New Brunswick: Rutgers University Press, 1965). For another application see Joel D. Aberbach and Jack L. Walker, "The Meanings of Black Power: A Comparison of White and Black Interpretations of a Political Slogan," *American Political Science Review* 64 (June, 1970), 367–388.
12. These issues are very complex and responses tend to be sensitive to small changes in question wording. The reader should be aware of this. The following sources discuss some alternative studies which have been conducted. Hazel Erskine, "The Polls: Women's Role," *Public Opinion Quarterly* 35 (Summer 1971), 275–290, and Connie de Boer, "The Polls: Women at Work," *Public Opinion Quarterly* 41 (Summer 1972), 268–277, show increasing acceptance of alternative roles for women, but show a tendency for many women to still prefer a wife-mother life style. For a study of abortion attitudes see, Connie de Boer, "The Polls: Abortion," *Public Opinion Quarterly* 41 (Winter 1977–78), 553–564. De Boer reports that "the percentage of supporters of legalized abortion has grown steadily since the late 1960's", but that the level of polarization is very high. The support-opposition levels in 1969 were 40% and 50%; in 1974, 47% and 44%. Also see Lucky M. Tedrow and E.R. Mahoney, "Trends in Attitudes Toward Abortion, 1972–1976," *Public Opinion Quarterly* 43 (Summer 1979), 181–189. Tedrow and Mahoney focus on six possible reasons for wanting an abortion, ranging from the endangered health of the mother to a decision not to have more children. They find support on all reasons has risen 3%–6% during the time studied, but that overall levels of support vary from 47% (no more children) to 92% (health of mother endangered).

13. *Gallup Opinion Index,* (Gallup International, Inc.: Princeton, N.J.), September, 1972, p. 15.

14. Crime also appears to be a major concern nationally. See, Hazel Erskine, "The Polls: Fear of Violence and Crime," *Public Opinion Quarterly* 38 (Spring 1974), 131–145. This summary article shows that fear of violence and crime is high and rising.

15. National patterns are summarized in Hazel Erskine, "The Polls: Control of Violence and Crime," *Public Opinion Quarterly* 38 (Fall 1974), 490–502. Erskine reports that most people favor policies of social amelioration rather than a crack-down, but that many people are losing faith in present methods. Doubters have increased from 56% in 1967 to 69% in 1973.

16. National patterns are summarized in Hazel Erskine, "The Polls: Politics and Law and Order," *Public Opinion Quarterly* 38 (Winter 1974–75), 623–634. Erskine reports a general shift toward a more conservative position on the part of all Americans, but finds that Democrats maintain a less conservative position than Republicans. In 1972 for example, 62% of Republicans and 51% of Democrats favored a death penalty; Republicans are similarly conservative in support for police, criticism of the Supreme Court, criticism of defendant rights decisions, and support for a pro-law and order candidate. Democrats are more pro-law and order only on matter of gun control (68% of Democrats favor; 58% of Republicans).

17. One interesting, if controversial, discussion of the "culture" hypothesis is found in Seymour Martin Lipset, *Political Man* (Garden City, N.Y.: Doubleday, 1960), especially chapter four.

18. National patterns are summarized in Hazel Erskine, "The Polls: Government Role in Welfare," *Public Opinion Quarterly* 39 (Summer 1975), 256–274. Erskine shows high levels of support dating back to the origin of polling. She speculates that polling may have begun just after a transformation of public opinion in the late 1920's or early 1930's.

19. See Hazel Erskine, "The Polls: Health Insurance," *Public Opinion Quarterly* 39 (Spring 1975), 128–143. In 1974 Harris reported that 45% of all Americans favored a comprehensive program and 28% opposed such a program.

20. The politics of environmental concern is an area that has received relatively little scholarly attention, despite the massive impact of environmental legislation in America in the 1970's. Because environmental protection may impede economic growth, Inglehart expected environmental concern to be associated with "post-materialistic" values, but his research findings ran counter to this hypothesis. See Inglehart, "Problems in Measurement of Value Priorities," a paper delivered to the IXth World Congress of the International Political Science Association, Montreal, Canada, August 19–25, 1973.

21. This debate is an interesting one. The revisionist arguments are put forth in Eduard Bernstein, *Evolutionary Socialism: A Critique and Affirmation*

(New York: Schocken Books, 1961). The Leninist response is summarized in V.I. Lenin, *What Is To Be Done?* (Oxford: Clarendon Press, 1963).

22. The Gallup poll in 1972 showed that younger voters were more liberal on all of the following issues: equality for women, aid to parochial schools, opportunities for minorities, national health insurance, guaranteed jobs, air and water pollution spending. *Gallup Opinion Index,* September 1972.

23. Paul R. Abramson, *Generational Change in American Politics* (Lexington, Mass.: Lexington Books, 1975).

24. See Miller, "Political Issues and Trust in Government," and Nie, *et al., The Changing American Voter.*

25. See Nie, *et al., The Changing American Voter,* Chapter five, for a discussion of recent national trends.

26. *Ibid.* Nie and his colleagues try to assess the gain and loss to the parties as they move left or right.

27. Erikson and Luttbeg, *American Public Opinion,* summarize this trend, p. 59.

28. *Gallup Opinion Index.* Erikson and Luttbeg, *American Public Opinion,* 239–241, discuss some of these trends. In July, 1970, Democrats were favored over Republicans as managers of the economy by a ratio of 44 to 29; in July, 1971, the ratio was 23 to 46; in August of 1972 it had nearly equalized at 35 to 38; by September, 1972, Republicans had pulled ahead by 38 to 35. *Gallup Opinion Index,* October 1976.

29. The *Gallup Opinion Index* periodically measures such perceptions. A 20-year trend is summarized in Erikson and Luttbeg, *American Public Opinion.*

30. See Miller, "Political Issues and Trust in Government: 1964–1970," for a discussion of the strictly political aspects of this trend. But other institutions, not just the government, have experienced a decline in trust. Ladd examined surveys from 1966 to 1976 and concluded that "every group of institutional leaders show a deterioriation of support over the decade." Everett Ladd, Jr., "The Polls: The Question of Confidence," *Public Opinion Quarterly* 40 (Winter 1976–77), 544–552, quote on p. 545. The 10-year figures for various sets of institutional leaders are as follows: higher education, a 30-point decline, from 61 to 31; organized religion, from 41 to 24; military, from 62 to 23; Supreme Court, from 50 to 22; the press, from 29 to 20; major companies, from 55 to 16; federal executive branch, from 41 to 11; organized labor, from 22 to 10; Congress, from 42 to 9; TV news, from 41 to 28 (for the years 1973–1976 only).

31. See Ada Finifter, "Dimensions of Political Alienation," *American Political Science Review,* 64 (June 1970), 389–410, for a classic demonstration of the distinction that sometimes appears between the two types of alienation. Her factor analysis of the Civic Culture data on Almond and Verba produces two dimensions: perceived powerlessness (lack of efficacy) and perceived normlessness (similar to lack of trust). In the present study, the

correlations were more mixed, with some trust and some efficacy items loading on the same factor.

Chapter 3

1. Herbert Simon, *The Sciences of the Artificial* (Cambridge, Mass.: M.I.T. Press, 1969), p. 99.
2. See Rudolph Rummel, *Applied Factor Analysis* (Evanston, Ill.: Northwestern University Press, 1970) for a discussion of factor analysis.
3. See Herbert Weisberg and Jerrold Rusk, "Dimensions of Candidate Evaluation," *American Political Science Review* 64 (December 1970), 1167–1185, for a pioneering effort.
4. Jonathan Kelley, "The Politics of School Busing," *Public Opinion Quarterly* 38 (Spring 1974), 23–39. Our analysis of busing correlates was first published in the *Michigan Academician* (Spring 1976). For a more recent analysis of national level data on busing, see David Sears, Carl Hensler, and Leslie Speer, "Whites' Opposition to 'Busing': Self-Interest or Symbolic Politics," *American Political Science Review,* 73 (June 1979), 369–384.
5. Angus Campbell, *White Attitudes toward Black People* (Ann Arbor, Mich.: Institute for Social Research, 1971); Gordon Allport, *The Nature of Prejudice,* abridged edition (Garden City, N.Y.: Doubeday, 1958); and Theodore Adorno, *et. al., The Authoritarian Personality* (N.Y.: Harper, 1950).
6. See Roger Cobb and Charles Elder, *Participation in America: the Dynamics of Agenda Building* (Boston: Allyn and Bacon, 1972), and Theodore Lowi, "Making Democracy Safe for the World," in James Rosenau, ed., *Domestic Sources of Foreign Policy* (N.Y.: Free Press, 1967).
7. Ronald Inglehart, "The Silent Revolution in Europe," and *The Silent Revolution: Changing Values and Political Styles Among Western Publics* (Princeton: Princeton University Press, 1978).
8. See Nobutaka Ike, "Economic Growth and Intergenerational Change in Japan," *American Political Science Review* 67 (December 1973), 1194–1203, and Marsh, "The 'Silent Revolution,' Value Priorities, and the Quality of Life in Britain."
9. Milton Rokeach, *Beliefs, Attitudes, and Values* (San Francisco: Jossey Bass, 1968). See also Phillip Converse, "The Nature of Belief Systems in Mass Publics," in David Apter, ed., *Ideology and Discontent* (Glencoe, Ill.: Free Press, 1964).
10. Inglehart, *The Silent Revolution,* pp. 99–100.
11. Murray Edelman, *Politics and Symbolic Action: Mass Arousal and Quiescence* (Chicago: Markham, 1971), p. 15.
12. Adorno, *et al., The Authoritarian Personality.*

Chapter 4

1. Philip Converse, "Attitudes and Non-Attitudes: Continuation of a Dialogue," in Edward Tufte, ed., *The Quantitative Analysis of Social Problems* (Reading, Mass.: Addison-Wesley, 1970), and "The Nature of Belief Systems in Mass Publics."

2. Our continuity correlations for Carter, Ford, and Reagan represent additions to the literature; our two-year correlations for Kennedy (.71) and Wallace (.59) are similar to those found by Converse and Markus, who report correlations of .72 for Kennedy and .68 for Wallace. See Philip Converse and Gregory Markus, "Plus ca change. . . . : The New CPS Election Study Panel," *American Political Science Review,* 73(March 1979), 44.

3. Our continuity correlation for party identification (.74) is again similar to (but slightly below) the C.P.S. two-year average for the 1972–1976 period (.81). Our results, as well as the C.P.S. results, indicate party identification to be the most stable, followed by evaluation of known candidates, followed by opinions on the issues. See Converse and Markus, "Plus ca Change. . . ," p. 38. (It should be noted that our party identification correlations are based on a five-point scale, while the C.P.S. study used a seven-point scale. Even such minor differences in question format can contaminate comparisons of correlations, so all comparisons must be treated with caution.)

4. *Ibid.,* p. 33.

5. *Ibid.,* p. 44.

6. *Ibid.*

7. Norman Nie with Kristi Anderson, "Mass Belief Systems Revisited: Political Change and Attitude Structure," *Journal of Politics,* 36 (1974), 541–591.

8. *Ibid.,* p. 43.

9. Our study contains 45 three-wave questions asked at one-year intervals. The CPS reports about 110 questions asked (with the same wording and the same coding schemes) in three waves with two-year intervals. Table 4.2 indicates that about 20 of these questions from the two studies overlap closely. For a summary of the CPS study, see Inter-university Consortium for Political and Social Research, *Guide to the CPS 1972, 1974, and 1976 American National Election Series* (Ann Arbor, Mich.: Inter-university Consortium for Political and Social Research, 1978). The totals of 45 and 110 questions refer only to opinion questions, and exclude background and demographic questions such as age, income and employment status.

Chapter 5

1. See Angus Campbell, *et al., Elections and the Political Order,* especially "The Concept of the Normal Vote" by Phillip Converse.

197

2. Arthur Miller, *et al.*, "A Majority Party in Disarray: Policy Polarization in the 1972 Election," *American Political Science Review* 70 (Sept., 1976), 761. Normal vote analysis was developed by Phillip Converse. See "The Concept of the Normal Vote," in Campbell, *et al.*, *Elections and the Political Order.*

3. The pattern shifted to favor the Democrats as 1976 advanced. Some of these patterns are discussed in Miller, *et al.*, "Majority Party in Disarray." See also *Gallup Opinion Index*, 1975–1976.

4. At the time of the 1972 election, Republicans were preferred to the Democrats as managers of the economy by a ratio of 38 to 35. By March, 1974 Democrats were favored by 49 to 19. *Gallup Opinion Index*, October, 1976.

5. Nie, *et al.*, *Changing American Voter*, p. 53.

6. Miller, *et al.*, "Majority Party in Disarray," p. 768.

7. The pertinent SRC findings are not directly comparable to our study because Miller and his colleagues included no entry for "Republicans" or "Nixon Republicans." They do note a "substantial degree of polarization" among the Democrats, but do not explicitly compare it to interparty differences. See Miller, *et al.*, "Majority Party in Disarray," p. 757.

8. Phillips, *The Emerging Republican Majority.*

9. The rank order of importance of variables is the same whether one uses the standardized regression coefficients from path analysis or the F statistics from discriminant analysis; and the sets of variables that give the highest percentage of variance explained (R^2) in path analysis give the highest percentage of voters correctly assigned in the discriminant analysis. For introductory discussions of path analysis and discriminant analysis, see Norman Nie, *et al.*, *SPSS: Statistical Package for the Social Sciences* (N.Y.: McGraw Hill, 1975). For a more detailed discussion of path analysis, see Otis Dudley Duncan, *Introduction to Structural Equation Models* (N.Y.: Academic Press, 1975). For a more detailed discussion of discriminant analysis, see Maurice Tatsouka, *Discriminant Analysis: the Study of Group Differences* (Champaign, Ill.: Institute for Personality and Ability Testing, 1970).

10. Our study, because it was designed as a panel in which the same questions would be repeated through the 1976 election, did not include questions on the Vietnam War. Since a number of studies have emphasized the importance of attitudes about Vietnam to the 1972 voting, our results must be interpreted with this in mind. Depending on how attitudes on the war correlated with attitudes in our Disintegration Cluster, our reported regression coefficients for post-materialism, women's liberation and busing would decrease, and/or the R^2 would increase. See Miller, *et al.*, "Majority Party in Disarray," and Frederick Steeper and Robert Tetter, "Comment on 'A Majority Party in Disarray,' " *American Political Science Review*, 70 (September, 1976), 806–813.

11. Warren Miller and Teresa Levitin also find issues important to an understanding of the 1972 vote: "The election of 1972 was the first presidential election in more than two decades in which concerns with questions of public policy were relatively more important than party identification as determinants of vote decisions by a sizeable portion of the electorate. . . . Even after party loyalties and perception of candidate issue positions had been taken into account, there was still a substantial variation in voting behavior directly associated with position on the New Politics." See their book, *Leadership and Change: Presidential Elections from 1952 to 1972* (Cambridge: Mass.: Wintrop, 1976), pp. 166 and 213.
12. In July, 1972, just before the Eagleton affair, Nixon was leading McGovern in the Gallup Poll. Their election eve poll showed the ratio at 59 to 36. *Gallup Opinion Index,* November, 1972.
13. Congressional Quarterly, *Watergate: Chronology of A Crisis,* Two volumes. (Washington: Congressional Quarterly, 1973).
14. *Gallup Opinion Index,* April 1973.
15. Several studies have been done of the media and politics. Two interesting Nixon-era studies are Michael J. Robinson, "Public Affairs and the Growth of Political Malaise: The Case of 'The Selling of the Pentagon.' *American Political Science Review* 70 (June 1976), 409–432 and Edith Effron, *The News Twisters* (Los Angeles: Nash, 1971).
16. Leon Festinger, *A Theory of Cognitive Dissonance* (Palo Alto, Calif.: Stanford Univ. Press, 1957).
17. For a classic application of this principle to political analysis, see Ole Holsti, "Cognitive Dynamics and Images of the Enemy," in David Finlay, *et al., Enemies in Politics* (Chicago: Rand McNally, 1967).
18. Converse, "The Nature of Belief Systems in Mass Publics."
19. These figures for our respondents were similar to national trends. The same three to two ratio around election time was reported in the *Gallup Opinion Index,* October, 1976.
20. See Charles Osgood, George Suci, and Percy Tannenbaum, *The Measurement of Meaning* (Urbana, Ill.: Univ. of Illinois Press, 1967). The semantic differential has an elaborate scoring technique—including a distinction between good/bad, active/passive, and strong/weak—which we did not employ.
21. The persistence and decline of partisanship in voting is discussed at length in Nie, *et al., The Changing American Voter,* especially pp. 47–73. Most election studies still find partisanship a key explanatory variable in spite of some obvious declines in partisanship.
22. David Broder, *The Party's Over.*
23. Douglas Hibbs, "Political Parties and Macroeconomic Policy," *American Political Science Review* 71 (December 1977), p. 1467–1487.
24. It is at this point—with these measures of voters' perceptions of candidates' qualities—that we move beyond the types of questions asked in the

1972 and 1976 Michigan Center for Political Studies national survey. As will be seen later in the chapter our best predictors of Presidential voting are (in addition to party identification) these new measures of images of the candidates and perceived character of the candidates. In comparison to our study, note the CPS's very general question on which man "has the kind of personality" a President ought to have; also note their two more specific questions about who "would bring high moral and religious standards to government" (which seems to violate a rule of question wording by mixing two items—religion and morality), and which man "could be trusted" as President. Miller and Levitin, *Leadership and Change,* pp. 214–220, and 275.

25. Brzezinski and Huntington, *Political Power: USA/USSR. p. 142.*
26. Don Kinder and Roderick Kiewiet reach similar conclusions in their study of voting for members of Congress. They find that such voting is influenced by (partisanly shaped) "symbolic" judgments about the overall state of the economy but *not* by personal economic misery (e.g., unemployment) of the voter. See their "Economic Grievances and Political Behavior: the Role of Personal Discontents and Symbolic Discontents in Congressional Voting," a paper delivered at the 85th Annual Meeting of the American Psychological Association, in San Francisco, California, August 26–30, 1977.
27. Miller and Levitin, in *Leadership and Change,* p. 62, report that in 1976 "the personal attributes of the candidates provided most of the impetus for Democrats to vote for Ford and the Republicans to vote for Carter." We agree. We here report a series of measures of voters' perceptions of the candidates not available to Miller and Levitin because they were not included in the S.R.C. questionnaire.
28. Stanley Kelley and Thad Mirer, relying only on pre-election data, correctly predicted 81% of the votes in the 1968 election, and do even better in some earlier years. Their results are not easily compared to ours. For one thing, they are able to make predictions in over 99% of the cases, whereas we can work only with the smaller group who answered all five of our predictor questions. Also, they rely exclusively on pre-election data. See their article, "The Simple Act of Voting," *American Political Science Review,* 68(June 1974), 572–591. See also the support for their approach in Michael Margolis, "From Confusion to Confusion: Issues and the American Voter (1956–1972)," *American Political Science Review,* 71(March 1977), 40–41.
29. Fred Lee in *Presidential Elite Support for the American Presidency* found that honesty was rated the most important quality for a President to possess, in a survey taken among 1976 presidential nominating convention delegates from both major party conventions. Respondents in Lee's study were forced to choose from a list of nine qualities, which only partly overlap with the qualities in our study.

30. Images of *competence* (in managing the economy and in holding down taxes and the cost of government) are two of the six significant predictors of the 1976 vote. This raises the issue of the relevance of competence in the 1972 election—and of McGovern's decaying image in this matter. Our study does not have measures of perceived competence in 1972, so we cannot draw conclusions about the effect of McGovern's declining image. But see Samuel Popkin, John Gorman, Charles Phillips, and Jeffrey Smith, "Comment: What Have You Done for Me Lately," *American Political Science Review*, 70 (September 1976), 799, and the other articles in that issue on the 1972 election.

31. See Gabriel Almond and Sidney Verba, *The Civic Culture* (Boston: Little, Brown, 1965), p. 14, for the distinction between roles, incumbents, and policies.

32. This party-image-issue order is also found by Boyd in his analysis of the 1956 and 1960 presidential elections; but Boyd finds that issues had some measurable impact. See Richard Boyd, "Presidential Elections: An Explanation of Voting Defection," *American Political Science Review,* 63(June 1969): 510.

33. *Leadership and Change,* p. 62.